A LONE WOLF STORY

ANDREW WILLIAMS

A LONE WOLF STORY

Forgiveness and Gratitude

Williams Publishing, Phoenix, Arizona

A Lone Wolf Story: Forgiveness and Gratitude
Andrew Williams
Phoenix, Arizona

ISBN: 978-1-7344428-0-9

Cover/Page Design/Proofing and Formatting: Carol Waltz, Bella Media Management, www.bellamediamanagement.com

Cover photo credit: EBFoto: depositphoto.com

Editor: Jan M. Whalen, MASL www.whalenvoices.com

Printed in the United States of America

To Flavia
for giving me
the strength and courage
to be myself.

CONTENTS

Chapter 4. EMOTIONAL BATTLES

Chapter 5. CONNECTING WITH SPIRITUAL SOLUTIONS

Chapter 6. BEHIND THE DARK CLOUD

PREFACE

THE LONE WOLF IS A metaphor I use to describe how alone I've felt in my life. Often, I've felt the weight of the world on my shoulders. As a child growing up in the atmosphere of a religious community, I was connected to a church's culture. I was connected to friends, family and the ideas they taught me about God. At 17, when I decided to no longer be included in the church community, I found myself cut off. I turned my back on what I knew growing up. It was challenging and sometimes I felt very much alone.

That was just a limited belief I placed on myself. Overcoming that limited belief is a life lesson I had to learn. I am still learning it today. Becoming a better person is a full-time job, as they say. Once you have gained an understanding of something, theoretically, doesn't mean you will always act accordingly. It takes serious willpower, discipline, energy and intention to act and to overcome our limited beliefs.

This book is about the journey I took to discover myself. I've been financially successful most of my life, but I still lived with anger, fear and I had doubts about myself and others. Why was this happening to me? Where did these panic attacks come from?

Why did I feel I had to bear this weight alone? I couldn't really put my finger on it, and I couldn't explain to anyone what I was feeling inside. I felt like I was exploding from the confusion and considered ending my life.

One day a friend offered me a piece of advice by sharing her story. She shared an opinion and the truth as she saw it. As I listened, a small light bulb turned on inside me and a vibration flowed throughout my body. This vibration swayed me back and forth, first slowly and then faster and faster. I felt like I was part of my surroundings. I wanted to know more about this world and myself.

That is when I began to record my discoveries in a journal. Much of this book is from the journal I wrote in 2019 where I documented my thoughts and the story of my life. I was hungry to learn, so I also meditated, practiced yoga, read and took classes. As a result, a whole new spiritual world opened to me. Some call the contradictions I've felt the Law of Polarity, which basically means that everything has an exact opposite. I am beginning to unblock the energy that was causing me to overthink the free-flowing universal truth within. I am humbled by this connection and excited to share my discoveries with you. Best of all, a whole new level of forgiveness and gratitude opened for me.

INTRODUCTION

*I started making money at
a very young age.
Dropping out of high school
in 9th grade gave me a taste
of what money
could bring to my life.*

EVEN THOUGH I'VE BEEN SURROUNDED by people all my life, I've always felt like a lone wolf. Back when I was young, I helped my dad do a variety of handyman jobs for Randy. Once we poured concrete for the duplex Randy built. My job was to run the concrete in wheelbarrows to the hard-to-reach areas. It was hard work and my huge boots always got stuck in the concrete. Shoveling and handling the wheelbarrow helped shape my life, not to mention the muscles of my young body that helped me with the ladies and in sports.

At 10 o'clock one night, we got a call from Randy. My dad said, "Come on. We're going to help Randy move a truck." Dad and I went to one of the apartments. There it was. It was an older 1980s single cab Nissan truck—nice chrome wheels and a cool gray paint job. It was a typical construction worker's truck with

4 cylinders and got good gas mileage. It was reliable with a cool feel and I wanted it the minute I saw it.

I asked Randy what he was going to do with the truck. He said he'd sell it like he did everything. He told me I could buy it from him for the amount the guy owed for rent—$1,300. This isn't a large amount of money but since I'd been researching the price of vehicles, I knew this truck was worth at least $3,000, so I told him I'd buy it. I closed my first deal at 15 and bought a truck even before I could legally drive.

Of course, since I was too young to drive, my older sister drove me around, but when I got my permit, I was able to experience the feeling of real ownership. Shortly after I got my license, my truck gave me that amazing taste of freedom.

What did I learn from this early experience? How does this help shape my money mentality? I learned that freedom to do what you want is sometimes a curse—the catch-22 of life. I had fun owning a truck, but the truck also got me into a lot of trouble. Looking back at this story, after 20 years of adulting, I changed my perspective a lot. I see how some of the things that just happened in my life back then helped to shape me into the man I am, and who I am today. This is true for all of us.

Most life lessons can be broken down when you write about them and look back. People can create a general strategy to follow in order to avoid major issues, pitfalls and traps that lead down an unhappy trail. I think how religion has played a part in my life. I feel that religion tries to capitalize on us at a young age by telling us the way we should live life in order to get into heaven and avoid hell. The contrast of hell and heaven played a huge role in my mind since I grew up in a very strict religion. Looking back, it seems like I've already experienced some of that heaven and hell.

When I look back, I realize I was taught to think a certain way by all my experiences. In order to break those up and dissect them like a scientist, I needed to find a way to be unbiased about my own life. This helps in all areas of life—not just money and religion. The more we know, the more experiences we have that haven't killed us, the more first-hand knowledge we have associated with that moment. Our memory. Our timeline. Our alternative dimension. How much would one decision have changed the outcome in the stories we tell ourselves?

Even though Dad helped me get this truck I would be jealous and hurt when he drove it. Rather than saying to myself, *He is my father and he helped me get this truck, so it's okay he uses it,* I got mad. I would yell at him: "Why are you taking my truck? I bought that. It's mine. And you're using it like it's yours. You need to ask me."

I learned to hold tight to that vehicle. It was my first taste of money and material possessions, and I remember having mixed feelings about it. I thought I needed them to make me happy, and those beliefs started to drive a wedge between my relationship with my father and other authority figures. I developed a bad boy, lone wolf, alpha male vibe. *This is mine. If you take it from me, I will fight you over it*! I didn't yet know how to deal with my teenage emotions and every new experience made me a prisoner to my ego.

I had to learn the hard way that how you treat people impacts your own life. The grudges that we hold make a huge impact. Most of the time other people are not as affected by our stories and negativity as we are.

I think about this memory of trying to fight my father over my first truck, and also of obeying the rules associated with the life of a fifteen-year-old boy. He was trying to help me become a man, to toughen me up by saying, "Don't be so sensitive." That phrase he'd say was like a mantra in my head. It was my self-doubt that led to a lot of internal conflict. I learned to allow a new way to breathe in darkness. I let the bad memories fade into the sunset of the majestic sky of my youth—one filled with potential until the dark night almost consumed me.

The feelings we attach to the stories we tell about ourselves are more than what any of us can imagine. We don't see the ripple effect it causes with our limited functions. We are blessed with the human condition in this life. Maybe people like Jesus Christ, Buddha, Socrates, Hercules, the ancient Egyptian gods, or even characters on TV lived well their whole lives. Our happily ever after only seems to last until the next tragedy emerges.

As humans we have a way of labeling everything. We put words and language around things to enable us to document our thoughts. But how can we really sum up the movies inside our heads with this linear flawed English language we have? We need artists, painters, photographers. We need poets, song writers, and musicians for all of our senses, and we also need pain to help show us each moment's impact on us. This is the human experience.

Bless the people who have developed their passions. The artists who are brave enough to see the world through their perspective, translate their feelings and emotions by creating beautiful masterpieces that give the colors of the rainbow new meaning. They pour blood-red onto a white canvas of the darkness. Artists enrich our language by adding symbolic meaning and depth.

Human behavior is just one of the many examples life uses to teach us. Life also uses animals, nature, fossils and data on the Earth to help shape our reality. We see huge examples of how large the galaxy is. We get that, and yet we don't know much about our own consciousness or what gives us the spark of life.

Life has a way of guiding us. My search to understand myself, to connect the dots, led me to journaling. I spent many months in 2019 doing just that, and I had a feeling I was going to share it with you. My intention is that you find some benefit in my journey. That's what this book is about.

Chapter 1

CONNECTING WITH SUCCESS

Journal

IN THE BEGINNING

"I WRITE TO FIND OUT what I am thinking. I write to find out who I am. I write to understand things." -Julia Alvarez

8/7/19 TODAY IS THE DAY after... After many life experiences. After many days up to today. 35 years for me specifically. Lots of life experiences in those years. Enough for me to be here now! In this moment, today, here NOW! Here as I write this message out for you! My mind, body, and soul have aligned to connect the dots. The circuits were built and today is the reward. Today is the present for my past trauma and a mound of experiences to date. The Present is a gift. The irony in the word is and always has been ironically pointing to NOW.

Born in 1984 in Phoenix, Arizona, I am the second oldest child of young parents with big dreams. I wasn't born into wealth, but I wasn't homeless either. I was lower middle-class bordering poor most of my childhood. We moved around a lot as I was growing up. Around the age of 11 we moved into a permanent house. I lived there until I moved out on my own at age 18.

I got my first real job in the summer of 7th grade. I was working for a church member who was an amazing wrestler. He was

1

strong, fun and in shape. He ran an asphalt company and because a lot of the older boys worked for him, I wanted to work for him. He paid great and was fair. I liked the stability having money brought me. It seemed to represent freedom at a young age because then I could afford new toys like my friends had. I can remember buying a new skateboard and a new pair of roller blades. I bought nice things that weren't hand-me-downs for the first time in my life. But just because they were nice and new didn't really make me any better. I wasn't very good at either sport, but it allowed me to be a part of the crowd. That was good for me because most of my life I didn't seem to fit in. You could call me a lone wolf.

I really became a lonely kid in 9th grade when I left regular school to be homeschooled and started working full time. Everyone else was out having fun and I ended up being exhausted from shoveling dirt and asphalt, plus doing my schoolwork each night. What I learned about being an adult was enough to get me to go back to school.

In 10th grade, I discovered wrestling and the competitive side of me started to develop. The friends I made in school and in sports helped to stabilize my life in high school. I wasn't a popular kid, but people knew me, and I started to take on a bad boy image. I developed the alpha-male, full of myself, hardcore image that I used to keep people at arm's length. The little success I had in wrestling and my years of working out in the 110-degree Arizona desert heat by shoveling asphalt taught me to work hard. Throughout high school I worked many long nights after wrestling practice to maintain my desire for money and the freedom it brought me.

Throughout the years of schooling and working I would also help my dad with projects he was doing. I remember being up on a tile roof as a young kid—being very careful not to crack the tiles. We spent a lot of time together as I would help him complete many different construction jobs over the years.

The summers before the 2002 Rodeo-Chediski Fire, I worked with my family to build a 3-story cabin that had tons of rooms for our large family. I grew up working. At a young age I learned to work with my hands in the construction world. I, of course, being young, was mainly the laborer. So, I never developed the skills to a master level or even a good contractor level. I was at the just-enough-to-get-into-trouble level.

This hard work was a good foundation for seeing what was possible when you build something. Sometimes I think the levels under the roads I helped pave taught me the most. Before the road was a road, I remember long hard hours spent running alongside a tracker pulling the blue sticks up and placing them back in the ground as the scraper moved dirt around. I ran up and down the Biltmore area in Scottsdale for a stretch of time in 9th grade. I was burning the candle at both ends with school and a full-time laborer's job. One perk while working so hard was learning to operate the heavy equipment. As I got older, I drove the water truck and helped operate the bobcat instead of the shovel. One time I brought my little brother Joey along. I must have been 16 or so and he was 12. I let him drive the water truck around and we made memories as we spent time as kids playing with real Tonka trucks and equipment.

After high school, I didn't really have a plan for my future. I wasn't going to college. I just knew I was going to get a job and work and that was pretty much it. I did, however, try my hand at becoming a paramedic for a time. I went to the community college and got certified as an EMT. I planned on helping people for a living as a paramedic or a firefighter. It would have been a great career choice for me, except it turned out I didn't like blood. I never minded seeing my own blood but seeing and dealing with other people's blood was too much for my stomach. After volunteering in the hospital and dealing with emergencies, I couldn't handle the pain of other people and the helpless feeling I would get.

I ended up settling for a job at Discount Tire, which felt more like what I was used to. But life got a little complicated for me when I found out I was going to be a father—then Ethan was born. I spent a lot of years trying to figure out this part of my life and how I fit into the mix. It wasn't until this year, at 35, that I started connecting the dots, realizing that I am more than just a work horse. More about that later.

During the time I was at Discount Tire, I was also training in garages with a group of mixed martial artists. We would end up wrestling around and fighting with each other as we trained for small-time no holds barred fights. I ended up realizing that

I was a great sparring partner in practice, but I had no business as a headliner. I didn't really like fighting, I just liked to train. I learned this the hard way as I do most things in my life. I ended up taking fights that I had no business taking. It inflated my ego at a young age and helped me develop the bad boy image even more. I found out I wasn't the type of personality that liked to inflict real pain on anyone. My short-lived amateur fighting career ended with a wicked car crash. The air bag went off when my left hand was at the top center of the steering wheel. It pushed my hand straight up and into the glass window causing glass to cut through two tendons in my two middle fingers. It left me with a scar that reminds me each day that I am not invincible.

The car accident had changed more than just my hand. It was a fork in the road in my life. My hand and my life path would never be the same. Life as I knew it was crushing me like a three-ton steamroller. I had to work all the time to take care of my child, even after the Discount Tire job ended, so I got a phone sales job while my hand was in a cast.

It turned out that the MCI phone telemarketing sales job was perfect for me. It was a commission-based job so the harder I worked the more I made. It fit my personality so well. It felt like the job I was meant to do. Why? I could really listen to the person on the other end of the line and connect with them, and if it would be beneficial for them, it would save them money on long distant phone calls.

I could get to the bones of what they needed and help them out.

A Lone Wolf Story

Many a time, I could get people to talk to me for hours. I was a super-star behind the phone. In front of people—not so much. It was an up and down roller coaster for me because while I was confident on the phone, I was also very shy in person. No large crowds for me. No way. It made me uncomfortable to be in the room with lots of people at a party having fun.

I moved up from telemarketer to a loan officer. I kept switching jobs and getting promotions. I was able to buy new fancy business clothes and I could afford other things for myself. For the first time it seemed like I was experiencing success. I bought a house. I had a new love. I was engaged to be married in 2007. I was making money and I was on a roll.

I was working hard back in those days and playing hard with my free time and friends. I was a newlywed man, and I had this nagging stress of needing to make money and work. But I also had the freedom to spend my day watching movies and playing video games or golfing if I wanted to. In 2008, for the first time in my life, I wasn't working so hard, I was enjoying what all the hard work bought me.

Too often people don't enjoy what they have earned. Success also comes with a bit of pride. I didn't realize that once I obtained success that I would have to continue to work hard to maintain it. Success sometimes is a double-edge sword and several times throughout my life when I would get to that point (in my eyes), I would let off the gas pedal and sit back and

6

drift. Turns out that drifting is a recipe for fun, but not so much for making money.

Between 2005-2009, I worked for many financial lending companies, like Ameriquest, Countrywide, Home Loans, and Stirling Home Mortgages. I was a lender for many states; I sold mainly on the East Coast where the time zone was three hours ahead of me. The time difference worked because that way I could reach people when they got off work. The telephone allowed me to shine. The internet allowed me to research market conditions. If you were working around 2007-2009, maybe you felt the effects as the economy shifted into a recession.

Like most people, I found my career stalled out. I lost the house I bought in 2007. I foreclosed on it and it sold in an auction for over $100k less than I bought it for two years prior. I moved into a rental and had to start over. I had my first real taste of financial turmoil and failure as I lost my career, my house and my pride. I didn't claim bankruptcy so at least I kept the cars, motorcycle, toys and family stuff.

Obviously, I hadn't made enough money to pay the bills when I lost my house in 2009. Was that my fault? Yes. It was my decision to let the bank have the house back. I had overstretched, chasing the American dream when I purchased the house in 2007. Yes, the economy shifted and the house was upside down. I (along with many other people) decided to let go of the house that was upside down and decided to start over. During the next several years I had to rebuild—over and over again. I have made money in the corporate world and have been successful as a sales agent and a manager, yet the frustration I felt from the pressure I put on myself weighed heavily on me.

MANAGING FRUSTRATIONS

I WAS KEEPING MY FRUSTRATIONS inside, bottling them up and smashing them against the pavement, all while running myself into the ground. I ran, rode my bike, swam for miles, and used the time to just be me. My body changed as I forced the pain of life to push me farther. I did this training with my best friend and at one point, we decided to pour our souls into training for a 2013 Ironman Triathlon that felt like it was going to kill us.

During this time, I was able to focus on work—on what I was accomplishing. I also released a lot of my built-up frustration and energy through training. I had to train like hell to get there. I sacrificed and found a purpose through working out again, and it felt great. I had started with small marathons to get back in shape, and to get my ACL back in shape that I had torn in a dirt bike accident. I spent my frustration pounding the pavement—and it felt good.

It kept me sane.
It allowed my frustrations
to wash away in hours
of exercise and work.
I found solace
from my constant disappointments,
in the exhaustion of my
physical and mental body.
It took me to the point beyond pain.
For several days and nights
my legs would be hurting,
my body would be hurting,
but I would be smiling.
The pain allowed me to feel again.
To feel the work that
was being done.
To feel the purpose.
To work through
the hurt and sadness
I had accumulated.
This also changed my body and
made me look better and
feel better on the outside and
on the inside as well.

THE LESSON OF THE IRONMAN

AFTER THE SUCCESS OF THE Ironman and the thrill of what it felt like to have a life purpose, what I was dedicating so much time to just fell away. All my frustrations emerged once more. The hours I spent training and the happiness I thought I would gain from this race didn't match reality. I fell into a confused and dark place. There had to be more to life than this physical pursuit.

The suicidal dark emotions of a bottled-up young man came back in full force. The accomplishment I built up left me broken, bitter and depressed. I expected something wonderfully life-changing to come from this accomplishment. It was a huge deal to me, and I thought it would bring me peace and joy. Looking back, I found peace in the training, in the preparation, and even during the race itself. But after I crossed the finish line, the accomplishment turned to dust. I wasn't happy. I was left empty again.

Here is the point. It's not just physical success and money that make us happy. It's all things. We must evolve and learn how to connect the dots, process information and strive for a balanced life. We can't be narrow-minded, greedy money hoarders. There is more to life than having money. The people who just dwell on money are not really any happier than a poor person.

Why doesn't money and physical achievements alone buy happiness? This is an age-old question and one I didn't have any good answers for. I felt that something was missing, so I spent the last several months writing, meditating, thinking, breathing, reading, researching, and questioning myself. I have found that this last year or so has been some of the most rewarding moments of my life. I am now more alive and connected to who I truly am.

Several things had to go just right in all aspects of my life for me to get here today. For the sake of others and myself I want to share some concepts and ideas about money to help others overcome this rat race and find more time to focus on self-care and on being happy. We have way too much mental illness, sadness and destruction in the world. TV news is terrifying to watch and and far too negative.

I have always been very careful about sharing my opinions on religion, spirituality and how to live life. I don't want to persuade anyone one way or another, and I still feel that way. However, I have discovered some universal truths as I have reflected and explored my life. I am going to spread my wings and expand my consciousness as I share my truth within these pages.

The way I see it. I find that I am happier when I'm in service of a worthy cause. One that I personally feel is worthy, not anyone else. Only me! I take responsibility for my life and my financial situation and my spirituality. Once I realized no one else will do it for me, I knew I had to. I had to let go and let the love of giving—something I've been doing my whole life—also be for me as well. That's what it means to have unconditional love for yourself. Maybe that is what Christ was talking about when He said, "I Am the Way."

PERSPECTIVE vs. AWARENESS

7/28/19 UNDERSTANDING VS. AGREEING. WHAT you read in this book is my story. This is from my perspective. Over the last several months many wonderful and new experiences have been happening. So many that it's hard for me to break them down and understand them all. That's why I began to journal them to understand myself better. I want to slow my mind so I can process them. As my conscious mind grows aware of a new perspective and new understandings, I need to trust in the journey and the process, and trust that I will absorb the information I need. I trust that I will evolve at the right time and eventually mature as planned. I trust that the road I am on will carry me forward. It's okay to stumble, fall, take steps backward, get upset and be confused. It's okay to take a minute to reevaluate what is going on and to want to take a snapshot of what happened.

Writing clears up my thoughts and
allows my thoughts and feelings
to get out of my head
so that I can process it all and
be ready for the next experience.
This book is about the practical need
to write down these new experiences
to process them,
integrate them and ground myself in them.
I want to absorb them and learn
what I need to.
Here and now
in the present moment
with the new awareness and
perspective gained.
I want to focus
on the right path and work
toward here and now.
As I am doing that for myself.
I'm hoping that my story
will help others start
to become more aware
of their own consciousness.

SLOW DOWN TO UPLIFT

7/30/19 REAL TALK AND REALITY check. Yes, I want to succeed, but what is the definition of success? All of these answers are felt instantly within me. I just took five minutes to write them down and it probably took you five minutes to read them. However, recognize that it took less than a split second in my mind. It happened instantaneously and simultaneously within my head. How many moments have we slowed down and truly dived into how that works?

I want to get a hold of this for myself so I can be a better father to my kids, son to my parents, brother to my family, husband to my spouse, employee/servant to the world around me, and spiritual person living an ordinary yet beautiful life. I want a life that inspires, uplifts and allows others to let down their guard and false mask. To feel/seek truth within themselves. To allow truth to bring light to the darkness. To let love heal the suffering within. To see that any moment can be a lifetime.

We live in a dangerous and scary world. Many are having such a hard time with their inner demons. They bring hurt to themselves and others. We are killing and hurting other human beings who deserve more. We owe it to the world to slow down and dive deep into the moments that are blocking our energy flow. The moments that have stopped the lessons we have agreed to learn and to distract and confuse us from our highest and best purpose that serves rather than destroys.

Our destructive and human flaws have led to horrible behaviors and actions. We have allowed ourselves to slip into the pain we feel inside, and it blocks our flow of energy. We must come together and slow down. I find it most helpful to look inside the moments that have the most pain—those buried the deepest. They may shake us with fear, cause anxiety and panic attacks, but most damaging, they block our true purpose. We must share our light with others. We must seek to identify the feeling and power of love we find within. Dive into our own truth and decide to stop being the locus and start being the servants. We must reach inside our own heart and pull out the gratitude, joy and love for ourselves and others. We must expand our feelings of love. We must double it. We must allow it to flow throughout all of us. We must expand into our daily actions!

I give myself orders: Stop crying in the bathroom behind closed doors. Stop the destructive behaviors. Stop abusing the substances that drown out hurt feelings. Stop locking away this hurt, sadness, guilt and pain. Allow yourself to be vulnerable. Bring up these painful memories and see them for what they are. Allow the light to illuminate more than just the pain you hide behind. Allow other feelings to manifest. Don't get pushed over by your anger. Don't let the more powerful "now" feeling dictate what and who you are and most importantly, what you do.

Here is a great exercise that allowed me to slow down, see the next layer, and become aware of the energy I feel. Journal your actions. Do a daily review each night. Identify the moments you feel the most. Identify the surroundings in the moment outside of your immediate focus. Dive deeper into the loudest feelings you have. Empower your imagination to identify where your energy blocks are. Identify and write down the thoughts you discover. Review these thoughts. Remember that old story: We all have two wolves within us. The one we feed is the one that presents itself to the world. Humans have the ability to consume and be a plague on the world. We also have the power to help heal and contribute to our overall growth. We are stuck in the duality of this world and we are polarized constantly—flickering back and forth between good and evil. Life isn't so black and white. Life has a lot of gray areas. We have a lot of limiting beliefs that have confused us. Set the intention to learn the truth. Set the intention to act towards aligning your life with your highest and best purpose.

MY NEW PASSION: REAL ESTATE

8/02/19 As I WRITE THIS journal, my intention is that it will be a book. I'm doing self-care and working to evolve and expand my consciousness and awareness. I am also still in this world making money. I am a real estate broker/investor working in many aspects of the real estate market. I have leveraged, borrowed, hustled and made deals work for win-win situations to create a life that enables me to make enough money to live comfortably, while having the free time to indulge and explore my other passions in life.

My real estate portfolio is set up based on short-term and long-term strategies that will one day allow me to retire with properties that sustains themselves. The properties I own and the procedures I set up to manage them will be a force that utilizes compounding interest and growth to create wealth to provide for me and my family.

I bought my first investment/foreclosure house in 2010 for $50k. This house enabled me to live with very little overhead as I worked full time, was earning my online bachelor's degree and raising a family. In my off time, I remodeled that house and created equity by modernizing the property. This was how I rebuilt my net worth. It led me to a love of real estate and the investment tool I used to leverage my time. I developed my ability to help people buy and sell real estate. I work with multimillionaires who own real estate portfolios that enable them to do nothing else but manage them. I also work with individual investors just looking to learn how to leverage their assets to create a cash flow that enables them to reap the benefits of monthly income.

I plan on working in the real estate business for the rest of my life in one capacity or another. I am passionate about it and I enjoy the lifestyle it enables me to have. Don't get me wrong. I have also had the privilege of losing roughly $130K in bad people investments. I was taken advantage of by a person who has been a plague but also a blessing in my life. I have purchased real estate deals that lost me money. But as with anything in life, the experience I gained both through my failures and successes has given me the confidence, knowledge and experience in the real estate world that will enable me to provide a comfortable lifestyle for those I love.

Chapter 2

BODY CONNECTIONS

Journal

OUR HOME

Our bodies are our temples.
Ancestors told us this.
Our bodies are our vehicles.
Our bodies are the robots
that allow us to experience
the physical world,
this 3rd dimensional world
of flesh and blood,
of life and death.
of heaven and hell
in the here and now.
We have needs that have to be met
in order for us to live.
The quality of the energy we consume
leads to the quality of the life we live.
We are all blessed with
the gift of agency.
Freedom to choose:
How to think.
How to act.
How to behave.
How to react.
How to move.
We don't yet understand consciousness
and our life-force like we do our bodies.

11/10/19 We are all blessed with a physical body. We are all born into this world under similar principles that govern our lives. Earth is the planet we call home. The body is where we place our conscious minds. Our life-force is connected to our bodies. Our breath is the energy that feeds life into us. Our bodies are the number one piece of the puzzle that we have studied the most.

The body is the unifying common answer that we use to gain experience. Our consciousness might live on after our bodies return to the earth. Some of us have had near-death experiences and have brought back information to be analyzed and researched. Some of us have experienced profoundly spiritual events that give us in-depth answers to the mysteries of life. Life is so big that not one person has summed it all up. But when it comes to this life, and when it comes to our bodies, we must make decisions and we must act on them or we will become stagnant and die. Therefore, our own understanding as individuals matters.

The shape of the body you are in is a story in and of itself. How you present yourself to the world says more about you than the words you use to express yourself. Your personal relationship with gravity speaks volumes about who you are. Science and spirituality play a role in this development. All knowledge must help create a life worth living. However, knowledge alone is not enough. We must also act!

Our body, mind and spirit need a direction and a path to walk. In other words, we are goal-oriented here on this earth. Our physical bodies are matter, and that matter is always changing. It changes according to our choices, and those choices have consequences—good or bad. We can get fat or work on getting skinnier. We can build muscle or have muscle atrophy. We can eat and digest food or we can starve and dissolve our own bodies. We cannot stand still. This is a universal law. There are so many options to choose from for physical exercise, it will take many books to outline them all. However, my advice is to pick one you enjoy: running, yoga, swimming, biking, hiking, snowboarding, golfing, playing with your kids or simply enjoying your physical life.

PHYSICAL CONDITIONING

WE ALL KNOW THAT WE must exercise our body. Our body is designed to consume energy, to function properly. Therefore, we must have a goal in mind and a vision, then set an intention. We can adapt and be the best version of ourselves that we can be.

In 2007, I tore my ACL, MCL, and cartilage in my left knee while riding my dirt bike. I was riding in the dunes of Yuma, Arizona. I jumped on my bike and was practicing wheelies standing up, because I'd just seen a cool guy doing it. This was the first time I'd ever stood to do a wheelie. It didn't help that I had a couple drinks in me and I was feeling good.

I got off balance and the bike tipped over to the left. Instead of letting down the throttle, like I should have, to stay on the bike, I panicked. I held the throttle down and put my left foot on the ground, attempting to push the bike. I didn't realize the momentum from the bike and the speed would not allow me to push the bike back over. Instead, my left knee gave way. The bike tilted to the side and ripped my knee apart. The bike ended up flipping over on me and I woke up in the camp, everyone standing over me asking if I was okay.

I ended up having surgery to repair my ACL. This was one of many self-inflicted injuries I have experienced in my pursuit of the adrenaline rush. I had to go through therapy, and I started to exercise to get my knee back in shape. I found solace in the hours spent running and exercising alone to recover. This solace turned into an obsession that lead me to running an Ironman event in 2013 that I spoke about in the last chapter.

IT'S ALL ABOUT FLOW

DURING MY LONG HOURS OF training to compete in triathlons, I learned a lot about the state of flow and the mentality I needed to keep going. Finding the state of flow in my training allowed hours to pass without discomfort while I ran, or rode my bike in nature, or I swam in the local lakes in a meditative state. I focused my energy to be in the moment. This struggle led me to a learning experience about my body. It was a haven away from the drama in my daily life.

The perfect flow is the place between boredom with the workout and having it be too hard. Too much will create overwhelming anxiety to the point of giving up. The flow is the sweet spot in the middle designed to keep you engaged and progressing over time. This is the most useful concept that can be added into all activities you pursue in life and not just exercise. But this balance especially helps with exercise, discipline and consistency. The best part of being in the flow means that time seems to fly by. What you are doing will absorb you and you will enjoy life more.

When I was young and competing in sports, I always felt like I needed to give it everything I possibly could. I would push my body beyond what was healthy. I would over-train and end up hurting myself. I would train in a way that made the next day difficult, but I would continue to push and continue to break down my body, because that's how I thought I was supposed to do it. After many years of torturing my body and calling it "training and fun," I learned to ease up a bit. In other words, I was not in the flow state but pushing past it and into the overdoing-it and training-too-hard-burn-out-state.

I learned the art of recovery through many long hours of training, so I could continue to train. I self-taught myself enough information to be dangerous. I am not a professional athlete and I didn't finish the Ironman in a record time, but I did accomplish an extremely difficult race. I was proud of competing in it. I witnessed people from all walks of life come together and enjoy the day. Many older ladies and gentlemen competed with me. I believe the oldest was 72, with an average age of about 50. It seemed like the fountain of youth was in everyone as they were all out enjoying the beautiful day—chatting it up and working hard together.

I also witnessed many athletes who had one leg, one arm, or who were blind, or competing to eradicate some disease, and many charity groups came together to support good causes. Tons of volunteers helped and a lot of people in the crowd cheered everyone on. It was an extremely special event that I was and am extremely proud of.

Immediately after the Ironman, I fell into the exact opposite state. I let myself go. I stopped running and training, and I started finding my solace in friends and drinking and partying again. I had given up alcohol for about seven months while I was training. I had disciplined many aspects of my life because I was still working full time and training while raising two kids. I had many responsibilities and directions that life was taking me, but I didn't have time for all of them.

I haven't worked out in the years since. However, I did just sign up to compete in the 2020 Ironman in Tempe, Arizona—seven years after I did the first one. I decided to sign up because I want to have a goal and focus on the physical area of my life. For me to enjoy this race, I know I must train, but I will train with a much different perspective now that I have the experience of having gone through it before. I am much older and hopefully a little wiser, and I know that it is about the journey not the destination. I know that I will have to focus every ounce of my energy to accomplish this task and I am looking forward to the challenge.

We all have a cultured attitude to train hard and push hard and go full out. But this mentality leads to short-lived careers and a huge burnout, or we become an injury prone person who gives up. We must change the mindset as we focus on exercising our bodies. Realize that the flow state is the easiest way to make exercise fun and consistent. Aligning our breath and our physical bodies to move in a graceful way is an art—one to be practiced every day. Our bodies and our lives are always changing. We must adapt and change with them. We must train smarter. We must focus on consistency over intensity. The flow is reached when we are in the moment, paying attention to what our bodies are saying both physically and emotionally.

In order to develop your ability to stay in the flow, start journaling about it right away. Remember how your day went and document common patterns. Identify what worked well and why you feel it did. See your progress as you are working smarter and identifying the connections. Prove to yourself that you are improving by the work you are doing. Time will fly by. Yes, you will fall in and out of the flow state—as we are all destined to do. Don't allow the frustrations to beat you. Set your intention and goal of what you want. Make sure it aligns with your highest and best purpose and work toward those intentions.

Setting your goals and intentions impacts the journey. We must have clear intentions of what we want to accomplish. However, we can't blindly steam-roll our way through life. When we have pain in our joints and muscles, we must listen. When we have fears and depression, we must ask why and where. The state of flow is more than just physical—it is mental. In order for us to stay in the state of flow we must be present in the moment. Prioritize and pay attention to how you feel above all else.

Every day before bed most people have a daily review routine. I follow Dan Millman's daily review. I focus on reviewing the day asking where I could have been more courageous in some circumstances, and then make an intention to be so in the future. I also review the day for love. Where could I have shared love, been kinder or offered more? Then I commit to do so the next day. Daily meditation, or some other introspective activity helps. And accept that getting into the flow is a continuous deal. No one stays there all the time; we always have to work at it. Everything in life is changing and the flow changes moment by moment.

BALANCE

BALANCE IS IMPORTANT TO REMEMBER in your activities. You don't want to overdo your training or exercising. I know people with bad knees who can't run or walk for long without it having an adverse health effect. So learn your limits. You don't have to go 150% all the time. The flow state is usually just over 100% of your normal pace. Find a comfortable rhythm that fits you. Then increase your rhythm to 110%. Move just a little faster. Many studies say 104% above your normal rhythm can have the perfect snowball effect you need to balance and maintain a healthy exercise—and this applies to all areas of activity.

For example, let's say you have 15 minutes of energy left during a game, and then you are done. During those 15 minutes, increase your energy output to 104%. This doesn't mean waste all your energy at once. This means take your average pace and push it just a little. Increase your heart rate just above average. So, in any activity when pushing limits, focus on the heart rate.

Don't tear down your muscles and overdo your exercise. So many macho men and woman go too hard and then burn out or injure themselves. Then they have bad habits of eating that catches up to them while they can't maintain the hardcore exercise they used to do. This is a bad balancing act. One that isn't sustainable. Only a few of the hardcore athletes can sustain this, but eventually they too are not able to sustain and must adjust.

DIET AND NUTRITION

Diet and nutrition are vital to a happy life. I wish there was a magic pill or a special diet that we could follow, but once again, we know so much about the human body and yet we are all a little bit different. We know that our intestines and digestive tracks are able to handle meat and vegetables. It's best to avoid processed meats and reduce the intake of food that has an expiration date longer than your life expectancy. As Americans it's good to eat less, but food for many is a weakness and considered a comfort.

Maybe this sounds familiar. When I am upset, I indulge in chips, bread products, fast food and cookies. This, of course, might be washed down with an alcoholic beverage or two—giving my liver the one-two punch. Ultimately, this leads to me overeating consistently. With over a year of doing this, my body will gain mainly fat.

You see, everything we eat and drink has nutritional consequences: The greasy pizza we overeat, washed down by the copious amounts of soda or beer, let our bodies know that we want to add pounds of fat. It uses the energy we have to break down and digest these foods. Often combined with stress and a panic, which leads to our internal organs not functioning properly. This is why we don't feel good.

I've learned this also leads to a lower vibrational energy. This snowball effect tells us, "Let's not work out today. We can do it tomorrow." The wrong food encourages us to sit on the couch and watch a movie. Then when the sun goes down, we don't go to bed. The greasy food we ate keeps us up and so we'll end up watching the whole second season of *Shameless* on Netflix.

What we eat matters.

GAME PLAN

Sleep is an opportunity for our bodies to re-energize and recover from the day. It is a necessity in life, and depending on your vibrational energy level and emotional state, you need more or less sleep. When I am depressed, I can sleep over ten hours. I simply don't want to wake up. And when I do wake up, I am tired and I don't really have the drive, energy or will power to make a change. This is a terrible autopilot cycle to be in. This is why most of us who are suffering from depression have a tendency to overeat and avoid exercise.

Knowing your body type will help you create a game plan that will align with your natural flow. Most people don't understand their Somatotype. Somatotype is defined as a body or physique type as introduced in 1940 by Williams Sheldon. This will ultimately help if you really want to have a detailed game plan.

It is unnecessary to know your exact body type, but it does help. Simply Google the three different body types: Ectomorph, Mesomorph and Endomorph. In order to identify which type you are, simply do a search online for Somatotypes and take some self-quizzes or watch videos on the different body types. You don't have to pay a trainer to come up with a game plan for yourself. All you have to do is slow down and do some homework. I know that's not everyone's favorite thing to do. However, if you want to have the best results for your body type, you should know more about Somatotypes and training programs specifically designed to help you achieve your body goals.

More important than knowing your body type, you must know how to enter the flow state. You must also know a little about your own metabolism and eating habits. Most importantly, you must know what calories are and how your body burns them. It's a fact that 3500 calories equals one pound of fat. In order to burn fat, you must have a caloric deficit. However you get to that caloric deficit is up to you.

Since most people either have a problem with food intake or not exercising, I would recommend starting with a very simple mindset: Eat less food at every meal. Stop over-eating first. Don't necessarily change your diet but learn to eat slower and listen to your body. Pause after you eat your first plate. Don't go back for seconds until you have waited. Then start exercising every day, even if it's just a five-minute walk or a yoga routine you do at lunch.

Competition drives us to achieve more and more. Because we're adulting, we tend to lose sight of the fact that life is meant to be fun. Children play and enjoy themselves and laugh and smile and cry and are in the moment. Many religions point out that we must be as a child to enter the kingdom of heaven. If the kingdom of heaven is here on earth, and the state of heaven is feeling gratitude, love and happiness, then it's well worth it to follow some of these life hacks:

1. Smile for a couple minutes to yourself
2. Fake laugh until you truly do laugh
3. Because thoughts can change the way you feel
—Imagine a happy time when you felt true joy
—Imagine a time when you felt extremely grateful
—Imagine a time when you were flooded with love
4. Breathe deep into your belly when emotions run hot
5. Play and dance like no one is watching
6. Find ways to implement fun into your daily routines
7. Practice perfect posture and stretch your body daily

Chapter 3

THE RIGHT FRAME OF MIND

Journal

2008 PERSPECTIVE

UP UNTIL 2008, MY JOB was amazing and everything was on a winning up-turn for me. Right until all the companies started shutting down and the crisis happened. Greedy companies, banks and lenders were taking advantage of those who owned homes. The market was going so strong during the years before the crash, it didn't matter to people. Everyone who bought an over-priced house saw that one year later, their house had appreciated 30%—sometimes more. For over five years we were telling people that their house would go up in value. People got the idea that money grew on trees and they leveraged it all. People didn't care that they just lost $15K-$25K in equity to the bank while they refinanced and pulled $80K cash out for themselves.

People didn't realize that the $100K they just pulled out of the house cost them more money each month. Why didn't people care? Well, maybe that isn't a fair question. They did care, but they weren't paying attention. They didn't pay attention to the interest rate on the credit cards they used to buy furniture, toys, clothes, TVs, cars, vacations. The majority of people used credit and over-extended themselves financially.

There were a lot of paycheck-to-paycheck people who, if a $400 expense came up—like the washing machine broke or the bar tab was too high—didn't have enough cash in the bank to pay for it. So the credit card with one swipe at 17.5% interest would cover that charge. It was the new American dream: the vision that you can have it now and pay for it later.

People were so leveraged they couldn't afford the lifestyle they lived. Heaven forbid they lowered their lifestyle. Why eat rice and beans when it's better to have Starbucks, designer jeans, designer shoes, and watches?

In a way, I never really followed the crowd. I was pretty poor growing up, and I didn't have the luxury of new clothes. I wore other people's hand-me-downs, whether from a yard sale or my cousins' second-hand sun faded shirts. I didn't really know any better, but most everyone around me did it that way. It became a way of life. Around the age of 12 I started recognizing that other people had nice stuff, and around the time I started working, I realized that's how they got the nice stuff. So, I wanted to make sure I had enough money to have the things in life that I wanted and enjoyed.

DISCOVERING REAL ESTATE

7/22/19 I TURNED TO REAL estate to reach my monetary goals and my first real estate deal happened in 2012. This wasn't my first real estate transaction, but it was the first time I had acted as an agent and used my license. This one transaction took months to finalize. I actually started the deal when I was going to school for my license.

At that time, I was working for University of Phoenix (UOPX) and had finished my bachelor's degree. I had improved the level of my day job, but I couldn't move past or increase my income other than 3-5% annual raises every year. I was feeling stuck. I hate feeling stagnant.

The real estate market was coming back, and I realized that it was a great time to buy properties directly from the bank through auctions, short sales, or foreclosed properties that would actually increase in value rather than continually decrease—like some areas had been in the past. Just like the house I was living in at the time. I purchased it for $55K at an auction in 2010. I saw the market switch and properties were worth more. If I would have had more money at that time, I would be very wealthy today. But I still did what I could to make an immediate impact on my life with the resources I had available.

One of my biggest lessons I teach: train others in areas where you are strong. By doing that, you grow in areas where you need help. When you work at self-improvement and make your job about growth instead of money, you will work from a place of love rather than a place of stress. You *can* make money and still get into heaven!

As a manager, I had helped train individuals while working my way up the corporate ladder. Mike was the person who influenced my life the most, as I helped him develop his career at UOPX. We were similar in many ways. He was a hockey player, liked the adrenaline rush and was fun to hang out with. He was a great communicator and had a natural talent for sales. His personality was confident.

THE RIGHT MINDSET

IN OUR WORK AT UOPX, the goal was a higher education experience. It was important to play on the strengths I knew Mike had. I somehow found it easy to "read" him. I played into his motivation and drive to improve his life. That's why, I believe, I had such success at sales. Besides, this is why I was going to school myself. I understood hard family relationships, hard life experiences and the drive to be better than an underpaid laborer with no hope of a better future. More importantly, I knew that an education helps people provide food/shelter/necessities that add to a better quality of life.

I didn't start off being the number one enrollment counselor, but within a year of working, I got promoted. I doubled my salary and outperformed everyone in the South East region—1000 employees throughout the United States. I excelled when I realized that successful people I talked to had gone or were going back to school. It might not be the school I was working at. Others went back to work their depressing job at a fast-food place, unable to get above it. I saw that most of the people from around the world (in this demographic I was dealing with) were the ones who had been handed lemons by life. My perspective was that they were trying yet failing to make lemonade. I use the word perspective on purpose, because it's key.

Without the right frame of mind and confidence in myself, I wouldn't have bothered to work that hard. My mindset made all the difference. I overlooked the high cost of tuition. I overlooked the low graduation rates. I overlooked most of the obstacles that would make almost 85% of the students who signed up fail.

I knew the statistics. I knew that most people don't make it past the first semester of school. But I also knew that the odds of them passing their first two classes and going on to the next class meant they would beat 80% of those who failed. As a bonus, UOPX paid me extra money for successful students—not just enrolled students. I learned the matrix that was to be my key to the game.

I signed up to win. The job I needed to do took 12 hours a day and sometimes four hours on Saturday. I worked this way for almost a year. I won't go into the personal troubles I was dealing with at home, and what I did to keep myself together, but I was damn good at my job. I would have fantastic conversations on the phone every day for four to six hours with individual students. I talked to them simply about—them. I would get to know them and where they were at in life: job, family, goals, and desire to overcome their stories. This was easy to do, because I seemed to sense things about them. And especially because the economy was pretty bad at this time. People had experienced tragedy all over the world.

Things were bad after the crash in 2008. Any available jobs had way too many applicants. Having an impressive resume with a degree started to become the norm. Before, a high school diploma and experience were enough to make a great living. That's when the economy was doing well. The people I was talking to were just like me. I was working at this job to improve myself and my education so I could be more marketable in the workplace, get a better job and make more money so I could provide for the people I was responsible for.

Getting to know people when they are in distress is easier because they are less guarded. People in crisis or panic mode are looking for a different way—a different path from the one that led them to the crisis they are in now. This is the cycle of life that we constantly overlook, yet it's one of the most important keys to discover our individual awareness—the consciousness that has been programmed into the subconscious autonomic nervous system. If you'd like to know more about that, there's a great book on the subject written by Joe Dispenza called *Becoming Supernatural.*

MIKE'S SUCCESS

MIKE WAS ABOUT MY AGE and when we met, we both ended up on the same team. I was his teammate/sales coach, so more or less I helped him develop his phone game. We all have shortcomings, and as I trained Mike, I became aware of his. For one thing, he just ended his hockey career and this was his first real job. I showed him how to build rapport by using his personality and I talked him through how to use the customer's words to phrase questions that drove back to the material he was selling.

It's not surprising he was very successful. He was the captain of his high school football team when he discovered hockey. He had enough talent to play professionally and developed the discipline to go after his dreams. He had a tremendous drive and thought it would be his forever career. His stars aligned in life until they didn't. He found himself not being able to make it in the league, partly due to an injury, and now he was looking for something else.

His story is similar to about 80% of the people in professional sports that I have met over the years. It's very sad to be around such athletic people who at one point had the world at their fingertips and had physically touched greatness in the games they were mastering. I'd had some athletic victories in my life—brief as they were—so I know what it feels like to be on top, to be the winner in sports. I also know the taste of defeat. It's a hard pill to swallow and one that leaves most people feeling like they're just not good enough. Sound familiar? More people associate with stories like this than I ever thought possible.

Mike became a manager two months after I did. We both stepped up to lead teams of people who needed training. Shortly after we became managers, the entire world at UOPX shifted. He was the last manager to be hired. The pay-structure collapsed in on itself, and the stock dropped. The government started to regulate the for-profit colleges and UOPX, or Apollo Group, was a huge target.

They were the Countrywide of the lending game that had just helped to topple the market. Countrywide dealt with subprime mortgages and the demographic of people who needed subprime mortgages—the lower-middle class, which was the majority of people. Do you see a pattern here? UOPX was not the best ivy league school, nor was it the cheapest. It was a subprime education with a high cost. The graduation or success rate was in the low teens. Why? Because their audience was the 25-50 age group, sometimes older than that. Most people had families and responsibilities. Some had messed up their potential when they first got out of high school and some still needed to get their GED to go to college.

The internet allowed them to go to school from home, with

flexible hours to fit their work schedule. The only catch was—and this was a big catch—it was college! You had to read, write and study to pass the classes. In other words, you had to spend sometimes 5-15 hours a week doing what we call homework. Who would have thought? Going to college to improve one's life took physical and mental work. In order to get this paper, you needed to pay for it too. Time and money.

Both of those were necessary in a day that averaged 16 awake conscious hours, often filled with a dramatic home life and nine hours of work, if you were lucky. Most of these people had to borrow computers from the public library and borrow a cell phone to talk to me. I felt obligated to do the best I could to help them find value in themselves. If they wanted to improve, I could help guide them in that direction.

The self-image I had was key to my success. I felt like I was helping them do what I was hoping to do myself. The only difference was that I decided to work for UOPX and get my education for free while getting paid. So during some of the 12 hours of work and six hours on the phone I was studying, doing my own classwork online. So I owe a lot to UOPX for providing me the opportunity to do that. It was a way for me to improve myself, and I am grateful for the hours I sacrificed to learn.

But the irony is I haven't once used my bachelor's degree in business management. The end game and goal had flipped on me. But to be fair, I did write a lot of papers. I did learn how to read and process information much faster and better than before.

I did spend four years online passing classes to meet the middle class standards of an education. What I realized after I got my education was that the corporate world wasn't for me—so I don't need the degree to open doors like I thought I did.

THE NEXT STEP

MIKE WAS ALSO A PART of the next step of my career. He had purchased a house because it was the cool thing to do. He bought a brand new home in a part of town that was improving when the market was strong, but not so much when the builder claimed bankruptcy and walked away from the development project.

So, he and I talked about the market. He knew I'd gone through a foreclosure and asked for my advice. I learned that he was upside down in the house he recently purchased and was struggling to pay the mortgage. I talked Mike into letting me buy the house from the bank while he lived there and didn't pay his mortgage. This didn't help his already ruined credit, but what did he care? He saved up about $10K and rented a new house in a better neighborhood closer to work.

This is when I negotiated my first short sale. I didn't hire a company to do it for me, I did it myself. I talked to the bank that owned the first mortgage and negotiated a price. Then I talked to the bank that held the second mortgage and negotiated a price. We settled on a purchase price of $126,500 for both. I was the agent facilitating this transaction, so I represented Mike. I was charging a normal 6% commission and splitting it with the buyer's agent like a normal real estate transaction.

This felt like a lot at the time because I was working and going to school—and this was my first transaction, mind you. I developed friends in the title department because I asked this really nice older escrow officer all kinds of questions. I developed a good relationship with my broker because I was performing a task where I needed guidance. I was stepping out of my comfort zone, but with the right help, I knew I could figure it out.

I was getting paid my commission, and it turned out I found the buyer to purchase the property. It was my (then) father-in-law. He stepped up to purchase the property based on my observation and the game plan I shared with him. He gave me a shot. He agreed to buy the property and had the cash to do so. Cash is king in this game. "He who has the gold makes the rules," as they say. I had to make sure the buyer was happy so when it came time to pull the trigger he would do so.

It all worked out. I was the buyer's and the seller's agent, so I got my first taste of being an agent who was paid 6%. Also, I made a deal with the buyer that I would fix up the property and resell it for more after renovation. So we resold this property on 3/29/2013 for $155k. So let's do the math on this.

The property was purchased on 1/7/2013 for $126,500 and sold for $155,555 two months later on 3/29/2013. It took about six months to make this deal happen. We started working on it in 2012.

Mike originally bought this house for $160,000 on 12/28/2009. On 10/31/2019, the property is estimated to be in a very hot real estate market. It's a sellers' market, worth about $260,000.

Mike was fine with what I was doing, mainly because he knew about how I lost my house. He knew that I purchased an older home in a centrally located area in downtown Mesa, and he saw that I had helped other people work out the financials on deals similar to this one. He also got to pocket months of mortgage payments while he found a much better place to rent. What did Mike lose? He lost his credit score. He lost the house that he had called home. He lost a part of his self-image in some ways, but also gained it back in others.

This experience was extremely stressful. It didn't all lay out as seamlessly as I've just told you. I had to spend hours on the phone with the bank to get them the paperwork they needed. It was more paperwork and homework than what I'd done to pass my college classes, but the experience I gained was worth more than whatever I made on this transaction.

Sometimes the best way to learn is by doing. That is what I have found to be true in my life. I can't sit back and wait for others to put food on the table for my family. Sometimes I have to be the one to do the work and create a game plan to ensure we are all okay. The success I found in this little venture has led me to work with wealthy people investing in the Phoenix real estate market today. The overall understanding I have of finances came from trial and error through my own investing experiences.

Today there are about 50K licensed real estate agents in the Phoenix area. Many of them do less than one deal a year. Most of them work part-time selling houses for friends and neighbors, making an extra couple of thousand here and there. Good for them. About 20% of the agents make about 80% of the money in this game. I've worked hard to be a part of that last group, and I continue to work hard to remain there.

THE RAT IN THE RAT RACE

It takes a trade to barter for goods without money. That is why money is the ultimate trading commodity. You don't have to be a welder to have an amazing screen door. You don't have to be an artist to hang art on your own walls. People barter. That is all the market and economy are, at least the way I see it now

But we can become enslaved to the work we are asked to do. I was addicted to making more and being successful. Why was I so addicted to it? Well, as the average American working for a dream, I wanted more. As I've already said, I wanted to have a better quality of life for me and my family. I wanted to help break the chains I saw holding everyone around me back from doing whatever they wanted to do.

We all identify what we see as success based on how we were raised, the culture we grew up in or our family situation. This is the story we all have in common. Individually we see it from different angles and perspectives. Your mind (or third eye or pineal gland) processes this information and you spit out a true or false answer like a robot. Subconsciously you are already programmed to think, walk, eat, work, relax, sleep, shower, and shop for too many items you don't need. To me, this is the rat race. There are many players on the rat race board. When I was 20, I read *Rich Dad Poor Dad* by Robert Kiyosaki and it helped to shape my opinion about money. I don't think anyone wins the rate race.

I was successful, the same way I was successful in running the Ironman, but still I was in the middle of the rat race. I realized being successful financially isn't enough. I found that I was wearing a mask, and underneath my mask I was angry. I was angry that masks are our normal. Angry that people say millennials are lazy. Angry that cell phones are so addicting. Angry that I don't have complete control over my own self. Angry that I haven't already figured out everything.

This anger was my wake-up call and my way of expressing other feelings as well. I began to pull off my mask to feel and listen to what made me angry. Just as I learned to do with my body, I knew I had to do the work needed to slow down, breath and examine these uncomfortable feelings. And that's what I began to do. It was an emotional journey, but in the end, well worth it.

Chapter 4

EMOTIONAL BATTLES

Journal

EMOTIONAL LIFE

Anger is an overpowering feeling.
It often takes center stage.
But the other feelings are there as well.
Sadness that people feel lost.
Sadness that I am angry and
not patient enough to allow things
their true course and time.
Hurt that I am not getting the entire message.
Fearful that I missed the important parts of life.
Fearful that I am shutting down
my immediate present moment
by spending time writing my thoughts.
Skeptical that my published words will be misunderstood.
Scared and overwhelmed that I am not enough.
Hopeful that by me letting my guard down,
sharing my passion and
my inner truth
I will help to create
a life I want to live.

THE MASKS WE WEAR

11/16/19 ALL MY LIFE, I have repressed anything to do with the psychic world or sensitivity to energy. I didn't even know about it. It has brought me a lot of internal pain in life. I never thought my level of sensitivity made me different from other people. I only wondered why I always felt like I was getting bombed with so many emotions. I always just thought of myself as really observant. I don't think that I am special. I think anyone can develop and pay attention to their psychic abilities. Maybe there are a few rare extra-talented people out there, and I may or may not be one of them. I simply take things very personally and in fact, realize am a highly sensitive person (HSP). I know that sounds weak and can be misinterpreted, but I had to overcome a lot to be the strong one who overcame my HSP nature in order to be the man I am today.

I wonder how many other HSPs are suffering yet they don't know why. I know all people suffer with their own personal issues. All people have pain. All people must overcome this to identify their own life's purpose and pursue happiness their own way. That is a huge piece of my desire to help people. I know that they may feel lower than other people and may have had to fight their entire life just to appear normal. That is the battle that I am talking about because I continue to fight to be normal. It's sometimes hard for me to function. Now that I know how to manage it more effectively, I can communicate with people without feeling so drained all the time.

Over the years I have talked with therapists, but I left feeling worse. Why? Why do people say that it is hardest before the light? Why does it get harder before it gets better? This is why: We have to go back into our memories and into our painful past. Why? Subconsciously we are blocking our energy flow that holds us back from the life we want to live. I remember my childhood—memory by memory. I sat down and went through my memories, being as honest as possible without exaggerating or expanding on the truth. Try it. It's not easy. It was not easy for me and if you have had hard times and dark emotions, it won't be easy for you either.

The other night, my oldest son Ethan and I stayed up to watch a great movie called *Split*. The main character had a split personality. He actually had 23 different personalities he would fall into: some of them needing insulin shots for diabetes, one was a woman, another a nine-year-old boy, a bodybuilder, a normal guy who was hurt as a child.

Long story short, he became these different people as the switch happened. Each one would hold the light for a short period of time. He dove into it fully and without judgement or cause. He ended up having a 24th personality called the beast. This beast was stronger, faster, better able to protect the hoard of people within, but did horrible things to humanity.

While this was science fiction, and the beast was an evil force, it reminded me that as humans, we have an untapped potential deep inside ourselves. We may not have achieved this big dream in the past, but we are becoming more aware and are able to tap into extraordinary powers within. Journaling has been helpful for me to unearth the various beasts within.

Events in our lives happen that take energy away from us, and some of us block the memories from emerging, which causes us pain today. That is why going to a therapist who asks you to talk about what happened in your past is hard. That is why being truthful and honest with others—especially yourself is difficult. I'll go first.

DARK EMOTIONS

11/18/19 DARKNESS, DEPRESSION, SUICIDAL THOUGHTS, anger, frustration. All of these energies boil inside me and want to be unleashed into something destructive—pain, sorrow, guilt, all of it. I sense all this—call me a sensitive. I am a low-level empath who takes on too much and am constantly bombarded with other people's energy. I am a lone wolf. I feel the weight of the world on my shoulders, and I feel I have no one else but me. When I do finally find a connection, it is ripped away. When I find love, I find the polar opposite as well. Life for me has never been a walk in the park. It feels good to let out some of the frustration and anger I feel inside.

I am constantly battling a back and forth internal battle. One minute I am on top of the world with a breakthrough, finding my connection to the divine relationship with the universe itself, with God and with a connection to all things. The next moment I am blocked, and the connection doesn't ever reach its full potential—leaving me feeling extremely disappointed. I am ashamed and hurt because I dared to dream that I could be more. I am on my knees with tears in my eyes. I clench my teeth, lock my jaw and squeeze every muscle in my body. Internally, I scream out in pain and agony.

Externally, I suffer in silence. While I present a false face on the outside, I suffer immense self-inflicted torture on the inside. Behind my false mask, I present a happy easy-going personality. I try to fool my kids. I try to fool my wife. I try to hold it together for people so that I can make money. So that I can be in this world and be a normal citizen and follow the normal path. But who am I kidding? I am only fooling myself.

The darkness inside me sometimes is so powerful that I can barely contain it. No, I have never truly hurt anyone; I have just enough control of myself to hold it together. Somehow, I always manage to run the pain away through drinking, working out, overeating, arguing with people who cross me, writing it down— in other words I have gotten through life transmuting the pain and the horrible guilt I feel into more productive releases that only hurt myself. But I know that I have also hurt people emotionally. I do so by the words I share when I'm angry. I do so by the way I ignore the outside world while I drift away into my unhappy place.

My darkness is real.
My connection to the darkness inside
hurts me and
brings me to my knees.
One might ask the why or where
of the pain.
I have asked both questions constantly
as I cursed the feeling,
like a lone wolf
howling into the air.

I feel powerful. Scary powerful at times. I feel like I can destroy anything: People, places, things. And yet I know I won't because I have a barrier. I have love in my heart. I know that I am just like a hurt child and that I am being dramatic. Somehow, I know that I would regret the actions I want to take. Why do I know this? How do I know this?

DUALITY

REALITY CHECK. YOU AND I are not so different! The pain you feel, I have also felt. The suffering you have put yourself through, I have also experienced.

Humanity is duality.
Evil and good both exist.
You can't have one without the other.
Heaven and hell exist,
here and now, inside all of us.
We all flash back and forth between them both
depending on the time of day.
Depending on how well we slept last night.
Depending on how well we are
getting along with the people in our lives.
Depending on the way we feel!
We are powerful.
We are creators.
We are more than we ever can know
in this human form.
Consciousness is yet to be fully understood.
We are blocked from the connection by a veil.
Our robotic brains and our robotic bodies and
our robotic human forms have an understanding
of more than we will know.

We are here to learn this!
We are here to choose the right.
We are here to pass the test.
What will we do when we feel the darkness?
The test is our life.
It is how we live when the doors are closed
and no one is around to tell us how to behave.
When our leashes are removed and
we are alone to make important decisions.
We must all adult.
We must all make choices.
We all must first learn how to function
in a civilized, cultured world.
We must all make a daily sacrifice and make money.
We all have a sex drive that needs to be balanced.
We all must eat.
We all must sleep.
We all dream.
We all have a hunger that comes and
goes as we consume energy.
We all have a conscious connection
and we are all aware.
At times we all connect to the message.
At times we all feel overwhelmed by ecstasy.
When we find love, we throw
caution to the wind and we pursue it blindly
knowing that this is worth changing our lives.

PATTERNS OF FEELINGS

I LEARNED TO FEEL GUILTY from the first time I felt lust, from the time I acted inappropriately according to the culture I was raised in, from the time I was told: "No, that is wrong. Don't do that." Or that it was inappropriate to feel that way and I should be ashamed. Well, I am ashamed. I am plagued with internal shame and guilt for the wrong I have done. For the times I should have said kind words and done good actions when instead I was rude or short-tempered or mean. I am ashamed. For the times I couldn't be the person others needed me to be. I am ashamed.

I am a hard person to get along with. I don't care for the normal things in life that sane people do because I am not a normal person. I am a lone wolf, howling at the moon late at night. I hear my wolf pack's calls around me, and yes, I find comfort sometimes in their ways. Yes, I find joy in running with them for a short period. But when the smoke clears and when the door shuts, I am alone. Inside I am holding the weight of the world on my shoulders.

I often feel like I have found a home, but then things change. The one constant in life is just that. Change. All things in life change. Nothing lasts forever. Each moment is a new moment and we are all blessed with the constant flow of time—evolution, truth, knowledge. Facts change. People change. Life changes. I change. My kids change. My parents change. My friends change. The body I have changes, and so does the way I feel. This darkness changes as well. So does love, along with joy and other emotions, but there seems to be a pattern to them all.

I now know that the pattern and the point of origin are very similar. When I ask, "Where do I feel the hurt, fear, or love?" it is usually from my heart. When my breath is taken away, and the adrenaline pumps through my body, and my energy is boiling, it all starts from my heart. My heart is the source of both the fear and the love I feel. Why is it so easy for me to feel both? This seems unfair. It is both a blessing and a curse. The curse is something I don't wish on anyone. At times, the way I feel inside can only be described as hell. I can't imagine a physical pain worse than this internal agony. I often welcome the physical pain as a distraction from the internal and dark feelings that are constantly bombarding me.

SPIRITUAL AWAKENING

THIS EXPERIENCE WAS A PIVOTAL moment in my life. It was pivotal because I was so desperate for a change, desperate for happiness again. It was in the middle of the day as I sat on the couch watching a show on TV. I found myself drifting off into my own head. I was pretty desperate for answers about my life at this point. I had been battling depression for a long time, and that depression came from circumstances that caused me to lose my sense of purpose and direction in life. The accomplishments that I had achieved didn't bring me the happiness that I wanted. I have had a lot of ups and downs, but when nobody was around, I was pretty sad. I bottled it up inside and I dealt with it alone.

I sat on the couch with questions that were driving me. Questions like: Is God real? Is this world more than just this life that we have? Is this all that life has to offer? If so, then I don't want it. This was the kind of desperation that was circling around in my head. Yeah, suicidal thoughts among them. I had known the despair of wanting to kill myself throughout my life—not just this one time.

As I was sitting on the couch processing my thoughts. I knew I needed a change—I wanted a change. Either something needed to be different in my life, or I was going to kill myself. I could no longer live with this feeling that I was getting nowhere. I kept failing at creating a happy life for myself, over and over again, and I was done with it. I was breathing in this pain, as if it were a dark cloud—a hurricane of anguish about my father, my religion, my failed relationships, my failures at work, even from my achievements and the lack of structure in my life.

As a self-employed man, I had to create my own schedule, rather than work a 9 to 5 job. When people control their own time, it's like having a long leash, and when people have more time, they can hang themselves. They really can. That's why it's good to be organized and have a structure to keep from self-harm or falling apart.

So in this dark cloud, with my eyes shut, I sat breathing in this darkness. I was starting to notice where the sensations were coming from in my body. In other words, I was feeling with my body, my mind, my soul, and my spirit. My heartbeat and breath were speeding up, and the hair on the back of my neck tingled. I was vibrating, feeling angry, torn, hurt, and tears started to roll down my face. In that moment I asked myself, *Is this it? Is this all there is?*

What happened next lasted just a few moments. I felt as if I could levitate. I felt as if I could turn the lights on and off with my mind. I felt as if the power was outside my body. I remember hearing airplanes flying overhead and birds chirping outside. I remember the noises around me coming to life. Behind my closed eyes, I remember the sounds and the surrounding vibrations.

I remember how a powerful feeling came to the surface. And I remember sensing my heartbeat and how it thumped in my chest. I could feel myself breathing in and out. Then I could feel my lungs expand within my body and the muscles I use to exhale. I felt the energy coming in and going out. I felt my heartbeat pulsating and speed up. I felt the power grasp onto my heart. I almost stopped my heart from beating, and I said to myself, *You know what, I don't have to live anymore. I can just simply stop my heartbeat right now. And I did.*

In my own mind, I stopped my heartbeat and within a milli-second, a flash came to me. A flash that questioned, "Do you want to die right now?" As I squeezed my heart, I didn't allow air to come to my lungs. There was a stillness of breath that moment and I had the feeling that I could die right then and there. I could just drift off, and know this consciousness, this power and con-nection. And I asked myself: *Is there a reason I don't slip out of this world and into the next?*

The answer and the reason came to me in the form of my chil-dren. I imagined the love that I have for them. That held me back. The message I received came deep within my body in the form of little gifts. The gifts were moments of love, of happiness, of joy. I felt little moments—like tucking my daughter in at night after a hard day. The power of this connection to her—my innocent child—and words cannot express the love I felt as I connected to that moment. The power that ran through me was stronger than my depression. It was literally the light at the end of the tunnel, a light that cut through the clouds of darkness. Little rays of sunshine came through as love. Love that I instantly knew I had for all my children.

The thought of them living without me in their lives changed that. Not my mother, not my father, not my brother, not my sister, but my children. I imagined them having to go through my departure and the trauma of not having a stable foundation for their future. I felt the hardships they would face financially without me providing for them. They would face emotional stuff without me being there to listen, pat them on the back and tell them it would be okay.

Why was this so impactful to me? Because it changed my life. It changed what I did in the moments of my desperation. The choice that I made was my own choice. It was my own choice to not commit suicide. It was my choice to come back and create a better life. First of all, for my kids. Knowing that I was going to be here, I needed to make a change. I knew I needed to get a hold of myself, dust myself off, put on my big boy pants, and focus on the bigger problems that I was facing in life.

I needed to stay because of my kid's financial security. It's not okay for me to let them down. I also needed to be around to help them solve any financial problems they might have in the future. I want to give them the opportunities that I didn't have growing up. I want to give them a better education and help make their lives easier. I want them to be able to achieve things that I didn't and find joy in that purpose.

Besides needing me for financial reasons, they'll also need my guidance in other ways: religion, God, who to date, who to love, and so many other variables in life that are hard and confusing. I want to be here as their rock—to be the best I can for my three children.

I knew that I wanted to be here for them. I also knew that I wanted to be here for myself as well, for my wife, for my family and for other people who are going through rough times in life. I wanted to be able to look them in the eye and give them a hug and be able to say, "Life sucks sometimes, but you'll get through it."

When I think about that life-changing day, I see my mind was like a dome, and behind my closed eyes it all became real. The power that I felt from this love connection was what I had hoped to discover as a child. Instantaneously I knew that this power was coming from me, and still it wasn't me. I knew that I could tap into this feeling and it could change my life. I had the control and I knew that my ability to connect to it was real. And yet when I tried to control and use it, the power disappeared.

I now know that all things are possible through love. It's the light at the end of the tunnel. We have all heard that story before, but it was me sitting on the couch, in complete and utter darkness, when the rays of sunshine flooded me with the gift and power of love.

What happened to me changed my life. It changed my mindset of how I approached things. It didn't fix or correct everything. I am still on that journey. I am not an enlightened all-knowing connected person, but simply evolving and living now with a deeper understanding of how much more there is to know.

THE RULES OF GRAVITY

I have seen some of the obstacles
that were blocking my life's path.
I have seen some of the principles
that can't be avoided in life.
I have learned some of the rules
that must be followed.
Gravity is something
we might not like, but we must live with.
We can fight it and argue with it and defy it.
But that is not going to help us
stay in one piece for very long.
This is a principle that we can't see
with our own eyes, but yet we feel.
We watch the effects of things falling.
We have labeled gravity as gravity.
We can study it in school and
we can do experiments in class.
We can study the effects of aerodynamics and aviation.
We can learn to fly with manmade aircrafts.
We can focus on the cutting edge of technology and
create a good life for ourselves
financially advancing our culture
as we advance how we fly.
As we advance our own relationship
with gravity.

VULNERABILITY

I KNOW THAT I WAS meant to share some of this darkness. I have an awareness or a sixth sense that has been nagging at me to explain my point of view to others through words. Why? Why would I want to let my guard down and show my scary insides? Why would I want to put on paper the ugly guilt I feel? Why would I want to open up and be vulnerable like this?

Well, the more I do it, the more awareness I have of myself. The more I let my mask down, the more I stop pretending to be a macho-alpha male who has it together. I also do it because I want to connect with my higher self. In other words, the more I stop lying to myself, the more I stop pretending that I have it all figured out, the more I stop trying to be normal, the more I stop shutting down how I feel and how I see the world, how I connect to people, animals, trees, birds and water—the more I find peace.

CYCLES

This is the cycle I am in now.
Fear is still there.
I just have to embrace it.
Anger is still there.
I just have to embrace it.
It is the most difficult task
I have ever ventured to take.
It is the hardest thing I have ever attempted.
I will never be 100% perfect at it,
but I must be honest with myself.
I know enough now about life
to know that I am not alone.
Other people, other humans,
also feel darkness inside.
Maybe they don't feel the same depths.
Maybe they have better coping skills.
Maybe they have thicker skin and
can easily feel both negative and positive
at the same time
while carrying out their lives and
are happy in the journey.

So the long and short of it is that I am alone and yet I am not alone. Life is an individual journey. My brain, my experiences and my body are mine alone. How I am feeling is mine. But is it really? That is a question that is plaguing me as of late. The answer to that question may be yes or it may be no. The truth is that it doesn't help me very much. Just knowing the answers to questions or having book-smarts doesn't make it easier when applying it to daily life.

The more knowledge you have, the easier it will be to make decisions. But the feelings and the emotions and the burdens and the hurdles and the obstacles are still there. They don't just go away because we know that they are there. Having the knowledge of God doesn't give you and God a personal relationship. Knowing that there is a devil doesn't give you an individual relationship with the devil. Just because we learned how to put clothes on doesn't make us a fashion expert.

Just because I can ride a dirt bike doesn't make me a moto-cross professional rider. I don't have the talent to whip the bike in the air or scrub a jump or do a back flip. It just means I am dangerous enough to hold down the throttle while going over a jump. The adrenaline riding a dirt bike is amazing—something I need. It brings focus to the moment.

THE JUMP

JUST LAST WEEKEND WHILE OUT riding at Ocotillo Wells, I took this double that was the biggest jump I have ever taken off a track. A 60-year-old pro rider took it first, and he made it look so smooth and easy. So I knew that if I just held the throttle down in second gear the bike would make it. Was I brave enough to do it? I said, *Why not!* So, I did it. I jumped that jump, and I ended up landing with my front tire just over the crest of the landing. In other words, I cased the landing just a little. But the bike bounced, and I stayed up and I made the jump. I felt excited, and I did it three more times, only faster. I was proud of myself, and I was amazed that I had the balls to do this. People riding with me also were impressed I did it, and my buddy wanted a picture. Of course, because I stopped to chat, my adrenaline and courage were gone, but I wanted to get a video as proof that I did it.

Well, with the next jump I didn't take off correctly and I was going too slow. I went straight into the landing. My body folded over the handlebars so hard I smacked my face on the front fender. The goggles broke. Then I ended up doing a superman over the bike as the bike and I both bounced up into the air. When I landed, my stomach was on the seat, and then I slid off the bike and onto my feet. The bike crashed, and I was in shock that I crashed with style. I landed on my feet and threw my arms up and screamed, "I am okay!" The next day I had some serious whiplash and my ankles and wrist were very compressed, but hey, life on the edge sometimes hurts. That's why it's called the edge. That's what makes me be in the moment. I bring this story up because I wasn't worrying about my feelings while I was approaching the jump. I wasn't crying about all the drama in life while I was hanging on for dear life. Another lesson.

IN THE MOMENT

IF ANYONE HAS GONE SKYDIVING, they know the feeling. Right before you jump, things come into focus. Right when you are doing the thing you probably shouldn't be doing, you are in the now. As you are free falling in the air you are present. Sports are wonderful ways to incorporate the Zen concept of being in the moment. I often wish I could stay in that moment. But we only can chance fate so many times before one mistake kills us off or leaves us with broken bones or paralysis.

There has to be a better way of dealing with life and the hellish difficulties we sometimes experience as humans. I am writing about some of the ways I am learning to deal with my own problems and my own fears and obstacles that bring me to my knees. I am not the only one who has been hurt. Everyone on earth has had difficult times. Everyone has internal battles. I am not alone in using substances to drown out the pain. Even if the substance is just food. We all know that prescription drugs are a huge problem for those with access, let alone the illegal ones.

I hope that I can help people realize that they are not alone, even if they feel that way. I hope I can help myself realize that even though people do horrible, disgusting, messed up things, they are all deserving of forgiveness and love. That is not an easy thing to say. I know a lot of messed up people in this world who I have turned my back on—who I have written off as bad people. I know what they did, and I know how they think. However, this doesn't mean that 10-50 years from now they won't wise up. This doesn't mean that I won't wise up. I am hard on myself because I have to be. I have a family who depends on me, and I have responsibilities that I need to be present for.

Sharing the pain I feel inside doesn't mean I am weak. Just because I am a highly sensitive person doesn't mean I am not also strong. I have an unusual tolerance for dealing with stress. At the same time, I usually take on more stress, so I have to learn how to handle it to function in life. This sounds like an oxymoron. That's because it is. It is polarized. It has both a negative and positive charge. This concept of the Law of Polarity has always been in existence, yet most people aren't really aware of it.

In this life we are all living, the universe has set up laws and principles that we must all live by. This can be learned and used to help us overcome the struggles we go through. We all strive to create a life worth living based on our own perspectives. The evolution and uniting of epigenetic (changes in organisms caused by modifying gene expression), quantum science, biology and spirituality are the way of the future. As technology advances, so does our universal understanding of these larger principals and laws of life. Even if you are not aware of what they are, you are always surrounded by them.

Despite the fact that we all mess up, and that we are all imperfect, we are all human. Sometimes human fear comes in the form of big dark storm clouds that encompass us emotionally and physically. These clouds can consume us and leave us feeling like weeping children, crying alone, not knowing and not truly understanding why. We are sometimes rushed with feelings that overwhelm our senses and our emotions and seem to take over the good intentions we have. This leaves us depressed and scared and shocked and unable to function normally, putting us in a panic mode.

Many great books have been written on the danger of stress to our bodies, minds, and yes, our spirits. Sometimes those who are highly sensitive are overwhelmed by storms others bring. These people take in the energy, vibration, feelings and emotions of those they interact with all the time—both on TV and in person. We take in energy from the stories we tell ourselves and from the stories we hear others tell.

We all have a mind that brings up feelings when we sense certain issues. Anyone of our five senses can trigger a memory inside our robotic brains. Our memory centers can recall a smell. For example, the smell of fresh sheets might represent a clean fresh start to each new day for some. Or the smell of an old book might represent the memory of hours spent daydreaming of better times. Or the sound of a firecracker or a helicopter might bring up memories of war for some, but for others it brings happy memories of fun fourth of July parties as children.

Our robotic brains and our memories don't always tell us the truth. Memories can't be trusted 100%. You can't even trust that you are aware of all that happened. We miss a lot during an experience, and since we are trying to recall memories, we are not being 100% present now. So, some of our energy is being used to recall the past. Some of our energy is divided trying to shift through the storm clouds. Often, negative, hurtful emotions are given the most attention because we don't want them. They are the loudest and most aggressive because we have the biggest reaction to them. Therefore, we put the most energy into them. It's another ironic thing we all do that we wish we didn't.

When an emotion or feeling or memory is triggered, either by us or by the storm of another, we shift right into internal memories. Our imaginations merge the memories and emotions of what happened in the past with what is now happening. This is a catch-22 because as we recall negative emotions, we lose track of focus. We introduce stress. We go into panic mode and we forget what it is we are doing in the moment. We are attacked by the adrenaline and chemical reaction these memories trigger. A scorpion, cricket, spider, snake, ex-spouse, or boss introduces us to memories that we associate with a set of feelings from the past.

JUST BREATHE

Breath is important in this time.
Why?
Because it gives the mind something to focus on.
If you can take a conscious breath of this dark cloud
surrounding you and consciously allow it in,
you will find that the cloud is not so big.
Maybe you breathe into this cloud
for about 90 seconds and
it is fully passed.
Maybe you breathe two deep breaths in and
you start to see the light
in between the dark clouds.
That is the sunshine coming
in between the storm.
Or you see the beginnings
of the rainbow as you breathe
into the fear that creeps up your spine.

I KNOW WHEN I FEEL fear, I stop and breathe into it. I recognize fear is coming from the same place in my body as love. My heart! I notice as I consciously breathe, my lungs slowly expand with air. I also notice that if I exhale all the air in my lungs to the point it hurts, the next breath feels good and fast and grabs at the present moment. That's because it is literally doing that. We must breathe to live. If you hold your breath or exhale, the air is replenished. This helps bring us through the darkness and into other potential fears.

Power felt in the darkness is the same power felt in the light. I often don't act on the anger I feel in the moment because I know it will cause more heartache. This is like a child who throws a temper tantrum. I can throw myself on the floor and thrash about, but if no one cares to pick me up or make me feel better, I must help myself.

If I am angry and lash out at the people trying to help me, they won't stick around very long. So, I must learn to control my behavior and have it battle out—manage it—internally rather than externally. I know if I take my fist and smash it into the wall, I will cause damage that takes time and money to fix, more time and way more money than I want to spend. So, the action doesn't justify the time and money—the consequences—of my actions. Of course, if no one is looking, I can break things and leave them for someone else to deal with. But that also weighs on my conscious. So, I might be leaving a mess for someone to fix externally, but internally I still must deal with the guilt and the shame of leaving behind this drama. So I try to think before I act and clean up my own messes.

SELF-HONESTY

BEING HONEST WITH YOURSELF ISN'T easy. Being a good person when no one is watching—integrity—is helpful to you! There is an amazing book on the power of truth, *The Four Agreements* by Don Miguel Ruiz. It's filled with easy to understand information that will help anyone. Even if you have read it before, it's worth reading again. One of the principles is *don't take things so personally.* I find this to be my biggest issue because I am my own worst critic.

I take things too personally all the time. When I mess up, I am hard on myself. When I hurt someone else or I make them feel bad, I am super hard on myself. I don't like to interrupt people's lives. I don't like to force my own opinions on them because I know how conflicted I am at times. Only recently I have been able to process my own emotions to connect the dots. The time I have spent writing and reflecting and allowing myself to flow has been good for me. It has been therapy in the highest and best form to write for myself to myself by myself. And of course, as I have shared some of my writing with others, it has validated my internal struggles. It has allowed me to see that people are not that different and that the stories we tell ourselves are all very similar. We are in this together, but we play this game individually.

A MESSY CONNECTION

8/15/19 YES, FLAVIA HAS BEEN telling me for years that I am messy, and she hates it. She is a hard-working woman, who outworks me every day. She has more energy than me. She is faster, smarter, and better at a lot of things than me. Especially when my default is stressed out to the max and I only have enough energy to do the work I am required to do for the day, and then after playing with the kids, I'm tapped out. I have to find new energy somehow or go to bed, but it doesn't leave me with the energy to be the most romantic partner. Or the best father. Or the best person I can be.

Do you get why I wrote how I feel? This was my default. I didn't recognize that I'd been super messy. And it goes back further than Flavia. My mom, in her caring way, took care of everything for me growing up: laundry, cleaning, food. I didn't even take out the garbage. There were so many people in the house no one noticed.

I always found a way to get out of cleaning, and some people I lived with saw this. I was disorganized and just expected someone to clean up after me. Maybe I was raised that way because the church put men first. Maybe...who really knows. For me, I was just unaware of the impact I was having even when people told me. I would try for a little while. When it was fresh in my memory. Then BOOM, I would get distracted for days or weeks, and go right back to my default.

I apologize to everyone. In an instant when I looked up at the counter and saw my mess, I got it. *Oh, damn, I was going to clean that up. Why didn't I? Oh, this is exactly like how I tell my son to clean up after himself. My eight-year-old son can't remember to put the dish in the sink! I had to be the one to remind you to put your dish in the sink. Me...The guy who everyone else cleans up after. Now I have to clean up after you! Seriously, figure this out.*

Yes, my son was doing what I've been doing! BOOM. The circle of life just happened. My son connected my awareness with how Flavia feels when she sees my messes. She feels like my mom telling me to clean up after me, over and over again. As a father who is spending more time with his kids, I see this. I'm the father who is thinking differently, a man who has changed his default from darkness to a little bit of light. One who can see the outer edges of other people's perspective more than just my own. I can sense them and feel them within.

IMAGINATION

I'VE HAD A POWERFUL IMAGINATION ever since I was a boy. I used to play with my GI Joe action figures for hours alone, making up stories and movies in my mind, daydreaming to myself in absolute blissfulness. I was often upset with anyone who brought me out of my imaginative world and back into the moment—like when dinner was ready. I was just fine with my action figures alone in the room talking to myself.

I often wish I could bring back this imaginary world, but I have to adult and I am responsible for more than just myself. I have been plagued with responsibilities since I was 19. I am responsible for how my behavior affects others. I have to be careful what I say because I can't offend people. My religious background put a lot of restraints on me, and I felt responsible for living that type of life for the longest time. Money became a responsibility and helping the family out financially at a young age played a role. Normal everyday problems needing to be solved came into play.

This pulls us out of our dream-like state and pulls us into reality. How we balance the internal wants and desires of our daily life is the spiritual game we all play. Even if you don't believe in God or don't consider yourself religious, we are all spiritual beings. We all play and live life with the same set of house rules. In the next chapter, I'll share ways I've learned to cope with the choices we have to make during the internal storms we face.

THE BUCK STOPS

The buck stops with you now.
As I laid out the ugly facts, I bared my soul
You witnessed the wolf within
You secretly spied on the beast—better left unfed.
I looked you in the eyes and said,
"You are becoming a man now."
Truth will come to you in many perspectives.
Half-truths heard from another truth of half the story
heard from the lips and whispers
gossiped from a friend sworn to secrecy.
As I look at you with tear-covered eyes,
you are grown now.
No more excuses.
You are a man now.
I can't be the one shielding you
from the bittersweet truth.
Congratulations.
You are a man now.
The buck now stops with you.

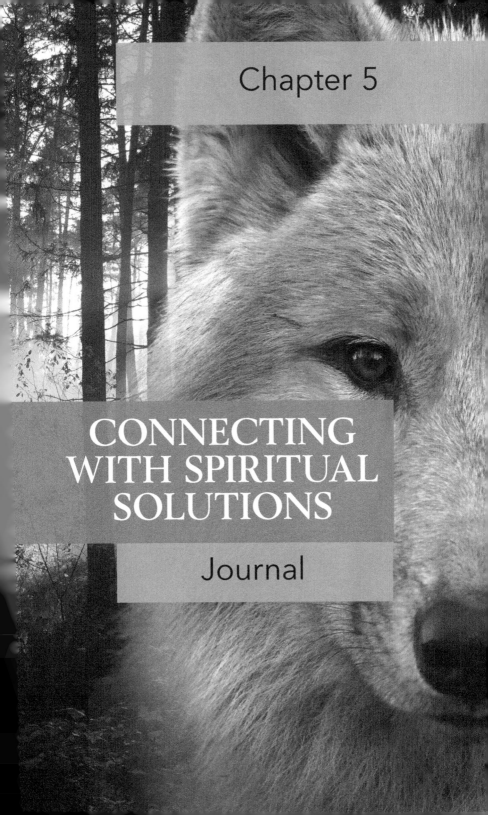

Chapter 5

CONNECTING WITH SPIRITUAL SOLUTIONS

Journal

THE STRUGGLE

I felt the pain caused to countless people
in the name of the righteous.
I felt the ripple effect on poor souls
who haven't found love.
I felt the loss and pain
that comes from feeling lost.
From losing our true self,
from confusion, loneliness,
and the scared childlike self
in a big world full of the unknown and
fear of the unseen around us.
At the same time the light within us
knows we can all get back to it.
The light that was blocked by birth.
The light that must be discovered within.
The evolution of our conscious and
subconscious minds emerging
into awareness of more than just us.

REALITY CHECK HERE! THIS BOOK doesn't clearly identify the steps necessary for you to take to become enlightened. This book is my journey and what I know.

We all have both good and bad experiences,
as well as some loss,
some hurt,
some pain,
some love,
some uplifting feelings.
Some good and some evil.
In a nutshell
we have
"choices and consequences"
because of our actions.
We all have experienced this world
up to this point in time.
Most of us have not clearly grasped life.
We haven't mastered playing the game
with rules we don't fully understand.

Most of us are struggling within. Most of us have a mask over our feelings, emotions, thoughts and inner struggles as we go through life, day by day. Some of us do a better job hiding it than others. Some of us take prescriptions drugs to overcome what society has told us isn't normal. Sometimes religious beliefs contribute to the struggle.

MY BAPTISM

I WAS BAPTIZED IN THE church of Jesus Christ of Latter Day Saints (Mormon) when I turned eight years old. This event was an extremely impactful memory from my childhood—but not for the reasons you might expect. I will simply tell you the story as I look back on this event.

The day I was baptized I had lofty expectations to fulfill. I don't think anything short of me seeing Jesus Christ, God, and the Holy Ghost coming down from heaven to bless me with a wonderful gift of knowledge would have lived up to my expectations. That may be an exaggeration, but I really expected something like this to happen. My eight-year-old innocent self believed my father and mother, who were quite religious, and I took what I was taught quite literally.

From a young age, my father and the church put a lot of wonderful concepts into my head. They taught me all about God. They taught me that I was here on Earth to serve. They explained that Jesus died on a cross for us all so we can one day make it to heaven instead of hell. They taught me that the Holy Ghost would help me, to prepare me for my baptism. They sat me down and told me I would receive the Holy Ghost in the name of Jesus Christ and according to the Melchizedek priesthood.

This magical event would bring the Holy Ghost to me. My eight-year-old mind imagined the Disney character Jiminy Cricket on Pinocchio's shoulder. The Holy Ghost would be with me from here on out. "HE" would help me choose right from wrong, and I would wear a CTR ring and forever be known as a blessed person who has a friend on my side to help me navigate the pitfalls of life.

I thought to myself, *Amazing! How wonderful it will be to have a buddy to help me.* So I listened well when they gave me rules to follow. They told me I needed to pray and ask God if I was ready to be baptized. They told me how I might feel and said I would see wonderful things at this special moment. I took it all to heart. I wanted to honor God and my parents and the church. I stood tall and I said, YES! I am ready and willing and able to do this work. I will be baptized. Let's do this!

So, with reverence, I prepared as well as a young man of eight could prepare. I fasted beforehand, prayed, read my scriptures, and put on my best church clothes. On the way over to the church, all my family members were in the car, but it was quiet and peaceful. No music, just us going to this special day where my father would baptize me.

There were a lot of people at the church when we got there, and my friends were running around having a good old time.

I remember wanting to play with them, but not today. I had to be reverent and good, so I was worthy of receiving the Holy Ghost into my life. My dad and I went to this special bathroom behind the altar where we both put on our baptismal clothes. I took off my tie with unsteady hands, and my father helped me. We changed into these all-white mechanic jump suits with zippers in front. They were giant onesies with short sleeves, and mine was a one size fits all eight-year old's kind of deal. They did not allow shoes or hair gel. Everything was to be natural and pure.

My dad explained to me what was about to happen. He said, "When we go through these doors we will walk into the pool. Then I will take your right hand and left arm and you will have to hold still. I will baptize you by dunking your head under water and then pull you back up. You will need to be completely submerged in water. If your foot comes up, or if any part of your body comes out of the water, it won't work, and we'll have to do it again."

So, the pressure was on. We were standing behind the doors ready to go. I was excited to see the Holy Ghost and welcome Him into my life and on my shoulder, so to speak. The doors opened, and we walked out into a room full of members of the church and my family who all came to see me on my special day. As I walked into the water, I remember seeing all my friends and family sitting on the ground waiting. Some of them watched me, but the kids played as if nothing special was going down. But most of the audience seemed as prepped and ready as I was for this miracle to happen.

My father blessed me, and he dunked me under water. It seemed cold. My breath was short and I was wet. And I waited with my eight-year-old expectations. And then it was over. I waited some more. I looked around, but I didn't see or feel anything.

My dad was still there, and I realized the white clothes were sticking to me and everyone was still watching me. I was a little embarrassed. Then we walked back into the bathroom and changed and went out together into the room again. We had about a 30-minute church session and I got to talk and play and the day kind of melted into just another day at church.

I felt the sting of disappointment because I didn't see the vision I thought I was going to see. I didn't get a buddy on my shoulder like Pinocchio did. In fact, not much else was different. But one thing seemed to have changed. I began to feel the emotion of guilt. I was ashamed I wasn't worthy enough to have a Jiminy Cricket on my shoulder. The bar of my expectations was set so high for this day, I felt crushed. The cracks in my belief were filled with guilt and I allowed it to pour into my heart.

Looking back on this memory, I want to give my younger self a hug. I want to tell him the pain and guilt he felt was okay to feel, based on what he had been told. I want to take him outside and away from everyone else and let him run around and play like a kid. I want to look into his eyes and tell him he is way too young to worry about fulfilling a grown-up version of the Spirit and that he is loved. And I'd tell him that someday soon, he'd realize that God has always been inside him.

LOVE: THE BEST MEDICINE

THEY SAY LOVE FROM OTHERS is the best medicine. Laughter is a form of love shared among people. Prayer is powerful. Why? Meditation is powerful. Why? Fasting and thinking on a subject is powerful. Why? It's because energy within each form is powerful. The thoughts and energy we give to this world is real. When we combine our thoughts and energy with others, we create a force. We create a large gathering of energy that is in sync and this energy creates miracles. It's a lot like playing tug of war. With one against 5, the odds are not as good. With 5 against 5 it is a 50/50 chance game. With 100 against 5, the outcome is clear.

Physical attributes are easier to see because our senses identify and prove their existence. Non-physical attributes such as emotions, thoughts and feelings are not seen with the eye. However, we all have them. Everyone experiences hate, fear, and love at one point or another. They are undeniable, yet how much time is dedicated to understanding them? Or more accurately, how much energy is used to ignore and block the feelings within. How much effort does it take to appear normal?

People do horrible things to each other in our world. They are

confused and they think they have it all together. Our govern-
ments, religions, society and communities have it all: the good
and bad, or the gray areas between the two. Why? Because
humans make up this mix. And humans are not perfect. Humans
are evolving. As we take two steps forward, we must take one
step back to evaluate whether or not we are headed in the right
direction.

LOOKING FOR PURPOSE

As I BOUNCED BACK AND forth looking for a sense of purpose, I was constantly in my head. I developed a type of autopilot life—a bumper between my feelings and the world. I pushed down all the sadness and pain I felt inside. I learned to distance myself from my emotions and I learned to party. I was free from the strict religious upbringing I had. I was free from the guilt I felt, free from their authority. I was free to run around and cause trouble. I carried an overwhelming, indestructible feeling. I was out of control and trying to find my own place in the world with the illusion that I was indestructible.

How many times
have you taken a step back
to look over your life decisions,
to reflect on your own personal
take on your life?
Not just what someone once said
you are good at,
not the stranger who said
you are pretty,
not even your parents or
loved ones
who know you best,
know the real you!
We all lie.
We all keep secret
our internal
thoughts and feelings.
We all repress ourselves
in some way or another.
We all are limited
by the language we speak,
yet we had to learn to speak.
It didn't come easily or naturally.
We were taught what Mommy meant.
We were taught about fear.
We were taught
HOT! DON'T TOUCH.

LISTEN AND SPEAK

JUST AS WE HAD TO develop and practice something as simple as speaking and listening to others, we now must develop and practice how to listen with more than our ears. We now must see with more than our eyes. We now must touch with more than our hands. There is more to this world than what the five senses can tell us. There is more than what is just on the outside of someone or something. As we analyze, learn, study, test and discover all sorts of things about any subject, we discover more. We are AWARE of more. It is work you can do today.

It would be good if we could stop our excuses. Stop the limited beliefs that we are not good enough. Stop negative thinking. Pay attention to life. Pay attention to what we tell ourselves. Listen for a change. Take a breath and realize that although everyone around us is breathing, not everyone knows how to breathe! Realize everyone has and is constantly struggling with their inner demons—with obstacles that keep them from learning more. These obstacles, these roadblocks, these energy blocks, these experiences play a role in the bigger grand illusion. Few have the stars align in the exact way necessary to see through their obstacles. Have this vision to see over the obstacles—see the bigger picture.

There has always been a bigger picture. Stop waiting for the right time to realize this. Stop trying to force it. You don't have to. You are already bigger than this temporary life you are in. You are already more than this mask you hold up for others to see. You already know deep within yourself that you are capable of more. Your subconscious mind, your body and your soul, and your conscious mind already possess the knowledge you seek. It is within.

However, just because it is within doesn't mean you are aware of it. I am not aware of it all the time. No one is perfect and good all the time. Everyone struggles with every new moment that presents itself. There are layers to this world.

Deep layers that we will start to see as we experience new insights. Right now this book is about my awakening. It's about putting together my thoughts and summarizing how I have gotten to the level I am at now. I didn't do it alone. I had instruction from many authors and teachers throughout my life. I've drawn on hundreds of experts—so can you!

We have the power within.
We have the power within.
We are the ones behind the eyes.
We are the ones breathing.
We are the ones thinking.
We are the ones experiencing
everything at the same time.
We are only aware of
what we decide
to be aware of!

Yes, there are guidelines and rules to follow to get to a specific outcome or consequence. There are actions we need to take to develop the abilities we already have.

ENERGY

Energy or prana is the universal life force. Energy can't be destroyed; it can only be transformed. Energy can be a tricky beast because sometimes things happen without us knowing they happened. Sometimes we see, feel, hear or do something, or someone else does something to us that takes our energy and focus away from the present moment. It's a world that we might not even be aware of, yet every interaction, and every word we say and hear affects us. This new information changes us whether or not we want it to.

To give you a very graphic example of this thought, think about the first time you saw something disturbing. Maybe violence in a movie. Can you unsee it? How about the first time someone really hurt you. Can you remember the details, and can you see the ripple effect it had on your life? How about the first time you had a sexual experience? How about the first time you saw something pornographic? What kind of impression did this leave on you? Have you followed the ripple effect this has had on your life?

SELF-HEALING MACHINES

We eat! We drink!
Our bodies turn the food we intake
into energy for our day.
Sometimes its great quality food
that makes us feel and react a certain way.
Sometimes we eat chemically enhanced
processed food that isn't the best quality,
and we still turn that into energy.
Our bodies are the best technology we have.
Glasses can enhance our vision.
Steroids can enhance our muscles.
Machines can identify energy output.
Technology has advanced beyond
what we thought possible.

OUR BODIES ARE SELF-HEALING MACHINES. When we get a papercut, it hurts. Our body instantly goes about healing. It does this whether we are aware of it or not. Yes, we can do certain things to help the healing process because science and common sense and our conscious minds have developed small ways to help. We can place a Band-Aid over the cut to keep infection out. Simple swelling can be reduced by adding ice. Casts can be placed around broken bones as the body heals internally. External medicine and care can help the body heal. Modern technology and medicine can give us peace of mind to help the internal healing process run smoothly.

My elbow swelled up in the middle of the day on Monday. It started hurting. I didn't hit my left elbow on anything, and I didn't injure it at the gym. That morning, I was actually playing video games with my youngest son and taking phone calls for work in between. Long story short, I ended up having a severe pain in my elbow.

Tuesday it got worse. I had visible swelling in my elbow that felt like I had somehow cracked the tip of it. I was also deep into the book, *The Energy Codes,* and was on week six review going into week seven. I had an excellent instructor, Moriah, who also teaches a Body Awake Yoga in Mesa. Tuesday morning, I called her, but when she didn't answer, I texted Moriah and told her my elbow was extremely painful. I said I am having a hard time today. I am wanting to go see a doctor because this pain is severe and yet I am struggling because I learned that I shouldn't tell myself a story around my elbow.

I learned from the *The Energy Codes* that energy is first blocked before it is manifested in the body as an issue, so I was struggling with my belief and what I should do. I was presented with a scenario where I knew I didn't injure my elbow by striking it against anything to cause a break. But I knew that it was swollen and I was in pain. I knew that I had many issues deep within myself that I needed to resolve.

The main issue that came up at the time was how to integrate my children, Ethan and Ryan, more into my life. I love them and want them to be happy and I want them to experience some of this new love I have found. I wanted to share it with them, but I just didn't know how. I also wanted to bring the family closer together.

I wanted to share it with everyone, including my wife and my mother. My nana was in the hospital and I wanted her to experience the knowledge I was learning. I wanted to integrate all these changes that were around me and make them a part of my life. This was the overwhelming stress I had, and I could pin down many others, but these were the main ones in my mind at my conscious level.

So, I fought with my elbow and decided not to see a doctor. I decided to do what I knew was right. My elbow was hurt and swollen. I knew I probably had a gout issue or a joint issue, like I had a year ago with my big toe after a wrestling injury.

After this decision was made, I went to yoga Tuesday night. Wednesday morning I had already scheduled an energy session with Briana, so at 9:30 Briana came over with her massage table and gave me an energy healing experience. I was skeptical at first, and just tried to learn what she was doing. It was a unique experience that I enjoyed. She concentrated on my elbow and she told me she healed about 50% of the heat coming off my elbow but there was more that needed healing.

She said I had a lot going on in my head and in my heart. My energy was blocked, and it wasn't flowing out my feet. She believed it was tangled up and not crossing over, and my head and the crown of my head were radiating heat. She recommended I figure out what was going on in my head and why my energy was in a panic mode. She mentioned a trauma could be causing this.

As we talked, she noticed that my little dog was very anxious and scared. This was a rescue dog, who was panicky and anxious around others. Briana tried to help calm her as well. She said if I pet and hold the back of her legs it will relieve stress from her. If I pet behind her ears it will comfort her and she will feel more at ease around others. She said I could draw a figure 8 (infinity sign) around her and others to help heal the pain and restore the flow of energy.

She showed me a stone she had that helps with grounding and calming while working through the energy blocks. Thursday the elbow pain started to feel better. I worked all week. Watched the kids. Took care of my responsibilities. Took some ibuprofen Tuesday and Wednesday. Iced my elbow. Talked to others about it who told me to go to a doctor. But I persisted in self-care. I took care of what I could. I rested in, iced it, tried to immobilize it. I also focused on clearing out the energy around it. It was feeling better and the pain lessened. The swelling got worse, though, as it drained from my arm it radiated an intense heat. It also turned red and looked like a bug bite gone wrong.

All week I was in pain and focused on clearing out the energy and tried to be aware of the subtle issues around it. I tried to convince myself that I shouldn't just heal the issue of the elbow or the evidence and symptom of the pain I was in. Instead I should focus on why I was in pain. What energy block was causing this within? What issue had I not resolved? And that is when I linked the kids and my feelings associated with them and integrated and grounded this into my new life.

It was a flood of life experiences. When I talked to Moriah about it, she gave me great advice. She said to focus on my central breathing. Three weeks earlier, Dr. Sue taught me to integrate this work into my life. This was about the time I was having all these new wonderful things happening, and she was kind enough to discuss this with me. She is a light that came into my life at the right time.

A few days later my wife, Flavia, and I went out for the evening with friends. I had too much to drink with no food in my stomach. To say that didn't work very well is an understatement. It was bad. Flavia eventually got me home and I was loud and angry that night—scary angry—and I lost control. I screamed in pain and punched the toilet in half. The water went everywhere. My elbow hurt—the pain was almost unbearable. I allowed myself to feel the pain and it came up from deep within. Deeper than my elbow pain. Deeper than the hurt and confusion I had with my father. Deeper than the pain I felt while I was arguing and saying mean things to those around me.

Pain so deep that it shook my world and caused me to lose

control. I went into autopilot for a minute because I was panicking. I was scared and my flight or fight mode was activated— no longer able to hold the mask in place and keep these feeling buried deep inside. However, I was still aware. I still knew I had made a mess with the toilet. I still knew I had to clean it up.

I went about cleaning up the broken porcelain. I tried to not cut myself as I picked up all the small pieces, but I failed. My hands were bleeding, mixed with the water, and blood-red pools surrounded the destruction. But then, as they say, "This too will pass." I fell asleep. The night was over. The pain was over. The memory was fresh, and I had to deal with it the next day. I needed to pick up my son, who left the house during my outburst when I lost control.

Then Flavia, Ethan and I all sat down to talk. I was honest with them. I told them how I lost control and how I regretted it very much. I told them I bottled up my energy and it was like in the movies when people explode with anger. I told them I was embarrassed, ashamed and deeply sorry, but that I loved them and wanted to talk through this and would like them to listen to the lesson.

Flavia proved once again that she has my back through thick and thin. She stayed by my side and helped me to build a better relationship with my son. Flavia really sees me. She is the one I spend the most time with. She understands me better than I know myself. Her constant communication and strong spirit invigorate me and help me be a better man. I am extremely blessed to have her in my life. If it wasn't for her, I don't think Ethan and I would have bonded over this experience. If it wasn't for her, I wouldn't be the father I am today.

I needed to talk through this with them and share the bond I felt inside. Luckily, during this time Flavia, Ethan and I bonded over this experience and this shared memory makes our family stronger. I asked if they could sense the change in me. They did sense it and sensed that I was okay. They noticed my elbow was not swollen at all and that I was clear, focused, present and connected to them both. We laughed, we cried, we connected more than we have ever before.

That same day I apologized to Ethan for not noticing how smart he was and how in tune with his emotions he was for a fifteen-year-old boy. I saw deep intelligence and love within him, and I felt proud that he was my son. I took pride that my boy came back and grateful for the way brutal honesty and truth helped us to see the love we all have for each other. Until then, Ethan didn't see under the mask I hold in front of myself. He probably saw me as a shallow person until I let my guard down.

Being vulnerable is hard to do especially in front of my children. However, when mistakes are made, we must stand tall and own our actions by taking responsibility and not lie or blame others for our faults. I took responsibility for my behavior and apologized for my actions. I asked for forgiveness and I allowed the family to help me recommit to being a better person for myself and for them. I am still trying to integrate this commitment into my life and make it a reality. My commitment grows each moment I can open up and communicate with integrity and honesty. I am excited to see what happens after this; I am excited for my life to have this open vulnerability.

PROMISES TO MYSELF

I am no longer going to repress my feelings.
I am no longer going to play the
sensitive victim I have played so well
for so many years.
I will stand up to my sensitivity.
I will face the pain within.
I will look at it and see the different views
that are present and
always have been.
I will see down the rabbit hole
to see the truth.
I will look through the veil
to see the light.
I will not be in this matrix anymore.
I will break these bonds and
slowly but surely find the truth
within myself and
the strength to speak and share my truth with others.
For myself!
First and foremost, this is for me.

All this love is for me.
Now!
In this moment,
taking the time to express and
share my truth.
In doing so, I hope to help others
who are going through issues
I have faced in life.
I want others to know and feel
what I am starting to know and feel.
I want to have this for them and myself
to look back on when life gets hard.
I want a light to grasp onto.
I am excited for the next steps.
I hope it is as glorious as my
internal gut is telling me it is.
I hope I can create beauty
out of destruction.

LET GO

IN MOMENTS WHEN LIFE BEATS us down, and we are at our wits end, our breath gets taken away and we don't know how to respond. There's a shock of energy to our system and we panic, and we freak out, and we stress, and we panic, and we freak out again. Science tells us that this panic is the death of us, that stress is overbearing and breaks us down over time. It blocks our energy and it clogs us up emotionally, physically, mentally, spiritually and brings us to our knees. Over time it kills us.

Focus on the present moment and completely let panic and fear go. The secret of all self-help books, religions and sciences try to teach us. Panic brings a stagnant hell and it comes with physical and mental diseases. It comes with shutting down our conscious life force and it blocks our energy. In other words, the panic mode comes with trauma that we don't fully understand. Trauma that forces our lives off-track. Many programs have been developed to help people identify the root causes of their panic attacks. The secret is to stop, to reboot the computer system. The secret is simple. The secret isn't even a secret.

We all are born with a self-healing body, yet we are all more than the simple flesh and blood technology we call our bodies. We have conscious and subconscious minds that can connect to a higher source. We are connected beyond the limits of our own conscious awareness. If we want to evolve and move past the life cycles we are stuck in, we must reboot.

The panic mode we sometimes find ourselves in is easy to recognize for some, and extremely hard to recognize for others. During my suicidal experience, I was able to connect to something higher than myself. It allowed me to connect back to Source and reboot my system. It was all about me recognizing that the limited beliefs I'd carved in stone over the last several years of my life were me lying to myself. The experience reset my life path and purpose and brought me back to neutral.

Since that time, I have been diving into my own truth. I have spent a lot of time researching other people's stories that were similar. I have read numerous books on the subject and watched numerous documentaries. I have spent hours meditating and thinking on the subject. I have found a purpose in life seeking this connection—many purposes. During my individual moments, my awareness has touched the stars and I've seen the bigger picture and theme of my life's movie. And for all that, I am still the same person, living a life surrounded by laws, rules, principals, theories, facts, truths, religions, people, occults, races, cultures and countries.

CHOICES

THE OTHER DAY I WAS talking to Tanner, a good friend of mine. He is a devoted Christian and a life-long LDS member who has dedicated a lot of his time to learn and grow within this religion. Since I grew up LDS, I have firsthand knowledge of the religion, but my experiences differ greatly from Tanner's experiences.

We agreed on several wonderful messages whole heartedly. He translated almost all of what I had to say into the way he had learned them. We were talking about the same thing but using different vocabulary. We were discussing God, or the Spirit of Christ, talking through someone, and other different beliefs that ultimately pointed at the same subject, with different ways to describe them.

Tanner made a couple of important connections that I would like to point out. The first big connection he made was one that many people will identify with. He said that the way he learned the things we were discussing is through the Bible, the history written within the scriptures he studied, and the religious teachings he has learned and studied. That same day I went to visit my nana in the hospital, she said the same thing to me. She said she gained her religious understanding through the Bible, and that led her to a place of peace within herself and her outlook of Jesus and God.

My comment to both of them was God is within. If we are able to look one layer deeper, we will find God speaks to us from within. And my thoughts are that this is one part of the same message. We have a power within ourselves that has knowledge we consciously don't know. When we follow the path, we find a way to do the work and seek knowledge, along with the healing presence of love. What is that called exactly? I don't know, but there are many interpretations of that throughout our history.

Tanner's second major point was this: Come home to your Master to learn. By that he meant we should stop listening to everyone who has a partial truth and start listening to the Creator and Master who is teaching it. He used an analogy from the time Jesus was resurrected, and that sunk the message home for him. I partially agreed.

He talked about the time the disciples were fishing and Jesus said, "Cast your nets on the right." And of course, they caught lots of fish. Also, later when Jesus was resurrected, he told them to cast their nets on the right again. Well, this instantly showed the disciple's that their Master came home, and they knew Him as the resurrected God. Why do I mention this story?

Well, I am not a religious man myself. I currently believe all religions have key messages crucial to help guide people down the correct paths inside every moment. My way of life is spiritual, and I believe God can have many names.

We shared, laughed and enjoyed each other's company despite our difference of opinion. We talked and we listened to each other's point of view without too much judging or trying to convince the other that we were right. It was a conversation in a restaurant after sharing a meal. We were communicating using the English language with words that were spoken, heard and interpreted along with eye rolls on subjects that seemed too far-fetched.

At one point I was talking about feeling the energy around the restaurant we were in and the power of choice we possess here and now. I made my point with an example. I simply reached over and knocked my cup of water off the table. (It was almost empty, so it didn't make a huge mess.) Instantly the room changed. Everyone stopped and looked, and I was able to make my point. Simply put, I have the power to choose my actions and whatever energy I put out, there are consequences to my choices. How severe the consequence is depends on our own individual interpretation of them.

Needless to say, since it was only a spilled cup, I quickly apologized to the room as I cleaned up the mess. Everyone stopped focusing on my distraction and went back to their own conversations, and whatever they were doing before I interrupted the flow of energy. Tanner thought it was a very rude way to make my point, but after a little explanation of why I did that, he got my message.

Before I knocked the cup over, I thought about the many choices I had to make my point. I could have simply explained my opinion on the importance of choices. I could have given previous examples to him of the power within the choices we make each moment. I could have discussed what an energy shift in the room feels like to me. I could have had him breathe deeply and walk him through a guided meditation to help him feel what it is I was feeling. I could have tried several ways to help him understand the message I was trying to get across. In the end, I went with my gut. I decided to show him an example that was off key but typical of my normal behavior. I decided to play it out physically as an example for us to discuss—and save time explaining.

This was a small example of how we all have the power to choose our actions each moment. Why not choose the ones that align with our highest and best purpose? Why not spend the time figuring out what that is for each of us individually? Why not do the work necessary to clear up our past energy blocks that have built up over time? Why not allow the energy to flow like a waterfall through us, splashing deep into the ground? Why not allow that water to evaporate through the air and accumulate into the clouds to be poured over us during the next rainstorm?

ZEN MOMENTS

In any sport there's a moment
where things slow down.
There is a shift in awareness
as the big plays are being made.
The last shot before the timer runs out
to win the game is important in a unique way,
and forces everyone around to pay attention.
The running back sees the end zone and
three defenders try to prevent him from reaching it.
The choice to move left or right,
to high jump or to brace for an impact.
These situations slow down time as we process them.
Practice helps us make the best choices.
We can practice this now.

We can meditate or create a practice
with yoga or tai chi.
We can focus on writing.
We can focus our thoughts and
align our intentions and
expand our awareness in any area,
maybe by a creative art.
We can design a beautiful sculpture
from a piece of trash or
turn a blank canvas into a work of art
with a simple paint brush or pen.
We can capture the essence and
energy that we see and
we can show it to others.

ENOUGH IS ENOUGH

MY LIGHT SHINES BRIGHTER TODAY than ever before in my life, and I'm finding new tools and methods to manage the memories and experiences stored within my head. I am now bringing my imagination from my past, future and present to open the door to the possibilities that await me. I am discovering the power within. I have felt a new stronger, smarter, faster, loving, passionate energy within myself and within others. I have felt this because I decided that enough was enough. It's time to stop floating downstream and it's time to figure this out.

Life has given me enough experiences, and I have tried and failed in so many ways. I now can combine what I have learned and use it to evolve. I have turned a new corner because I now have the discipline, desire, and will-power to do so. Why? Because the timing is right. The obstacles I put in front of me are no longer so big. I have experienced enough pain for ten lifetimes. I have experienced enough hate, and I know the depth of suicidal thoughts. I have had enough sadness and fear to know the beauty of love. Enough is enough at this point. I have found the strength and willpower to act.

This is what I tell myself: Do the work. Stop making excuses. Stop blocking yourself. Stop allowing your mind to get in your way. Stop listening to skeptics around you, you're good enough. Stop the drama and get it done. Too often we tell ourselves lies and give excuses that prevent us from moving forward. Well, life is meant to be lived. We are here now for a purpose—maybe more than one. Those purposes, both big and small, are important. It is important to identify our strengths and the obstacles standing in our way. Self-realization is what we're talking about here.

As the Terminator once said, "I'll be back!" And he was right, because they made several terminator movies—all huge hits. The Terminator's life goes on, as well as our lives. We keep coming back. We can only stop and smell the roses occasionally. We can only pause to write down our deepest inner thoughts once in a while. The part I like about journaling is that it's random and I'm not sure what I'll say until I've written it. Journaling is like bringing the past back to make sense of the present.

FREE-FLOW JOURNALING

10/23/19 THERE IS ONLY ONE story! Whose story is it? It's your story! What is the story? The one you have been telling yourself from the beginning of time! Or from the beginning of birth? Maybe yes and maybe no.

Why the topic of story today? Well, I have been thinking a lot about the workshop I took a couple weeks ago with Sue Morter. I have been contemplating the new discovery that I had. I have been questioning what happened to me at her event. I talked about it out loud on a podcast on the way home.

I had been sitting outside waiting for about two hours after the event. Waiting for what? I wasn't sure. Waiting for an answer to my questions. Waiting for the voice inside my head to connect the dots. Waiting for a great editor to come and help me translate the scrambled messages I have been receiving. Waiting for someone to come along and organize, help process, descramble the illusion, to put the puzzle together that I have built. The puzzle pieces are screen shots that I have consciously remembered and pieced out over time. How much time? That is a great question.

Journaling questions through a stream-of-consciousness format and I wait for the answers to come to me. Is that really enough? Well, if one story is mine and mine alone, then I think the answer is yes! Absolutely, my opinion is the only one that truly matters.

Matter is an interesting word. Are we all just matter? Or are we more? Where is our consciousness coming from? Subconsciousness? GOD? Source? Jesus Christ? Holy Ghost? Buddha? "I don't know" is what comes out first, and then practical answers come to me from all my questions. And the best question of all: Who determines that my answer is better than yours?

We only have two eyes to see all that we see, right? Well, not quite. We also have a third eye. Some call it a 6th sense or a spirit guide or the light of Christ or a Jiminy Cricket sitting on your shoulder saying hmmmmmm? Oh, I see! Maybe the second puberty that I have been experiencing is the voice inside me talking constantly. Maybe, I am my own Jiminy Cricket. Maybe when I was baptized, I thought I'd see the Holy Ghost. I just didn't really understand the impact of the third eye at that time.

Maybe I wasn't ready to grasp the full understanding of the power we possess internally. Now that I have consciously witnessed life unfolding for 35 years, I have had enough go wrong to learn that I need to take responsibility for my own story!

I have been reading Dan Milliman since I was 15. His advice and his recent books have played a huge role in my life. I am now reading Joe Dispensa's book, *Becoming Supernatural,* and watching his TV series called *Rewired*. Yes, the friend who opened up about God and how she knows him personally helped me tremendously. Yes, my wife, who I spend the most time with has influenced me on a daily, sometimes moment by moment basis. Who you read and who you spend your time with has a direct reflection on you. Why? Because of the one-story concept. Because we are ultimately part of the one consciousness. Our heart's intelligence and magnetic energy radiate into the universe.

SEE YOUR LIFE

We are the heartbeat of the Universe.
We are connected and
more people are waking up
to this realization every day.
Open your eyes.
Step outside of your comfort zone.
Make an impact on your life and
the lives of others today!
Right now.
Not because someone told you so.
For no reason other than you want to.
Be that change,
Make a meaningful sacrifice!
What in your life do you want to improve?

MY GOOD FRIEND SENT A bumper sticker to me yesterday that said: "You are over complicating it." Keep it simple! WOW.

THE STORIES WE TELL OURSELVES

10/31/19 STORIES CARRY THE EMOTIONS we store in our memories. When our mind searches for the story, it senses the melody or pitch or vibrational frequency stored in the memory sections: bad feelings, anger, hurt, guilt, failure, pain, fear. The memory center also stores things in the love files: truth, religion, family love, self-love, self-image, God, gratitude, humility, feelings that everything will be okay, we are one, and we don't have to compete here.

What happens is that as we bounce around in search of our memories, we add to our feelings. If we remember the negative and the bad, we will associate more stories with bad emotions, and block them from flowing out. The more open we are to seeing the bright side of the journey, the better. Unconditional love for ourselves is more important than having a mask—we will even be better in balance. We will activate more areas of our brain and unify more of our intelligence and energy surging through us already. In other words, we will be unblocking clogged energy simply by remembering the story and the truth more clearly.

This is why the stories we tell ourselves or others about a situation we experienced firsthand are important to communication.

Magic lives within our words. The words we use when talking about ourselves and others around us are a huge indicator of our self-image. Sometimes we need to overcome our story. If our stories include words like "You need to be more patient with me, I am trying here!", then we need to look in a mirror and say it again. But this time answer back with an "Okay! I will do just that. I know I might fail, and I am not perfect, but no one is."

Life is the spiritual movie we need to stand up and rewrite. We have time. All of us are the authors of our own lives. We need to remember to fill our own cups first before handing it to others. Or better yet, as Sue Morter says, "Allow your cup to fill up and overflow into the saucer below. Let the cup be for you and the saucer for others. That way you are always full." I have heard this same concept my entire life, but for some reason it makes more sense today.

I saw another perspective on how I am writing my own story. I saw how connected I was to the 150 people at the workshop that day. Many were older and still questioning who they were. Some younger, who will shape this world in the future. Generations are coming and going. Life is cycling in many areas and it's all one big game with rules we must learn so we can win. This leads me to quantum science and how that plays into what I am doing.

QUANTUM SCIENCE

QUANTUM SCIENCE DEALS WITH THE smallest amount of any physical entity. It's all about energy and its influence on how energy and matter interact. It helps us understand and describe nature. Vibrations of energy take place automatically even if we are not aware of them. So what happens when we become aware of the world around us? What I find interesting is that quantum science is proving spiritual concepts are pretty accurate. The chakra systems and the meridian lines in the body are matching up to our energy lines.

Consciousness is one of the least understood aspect of the human experience. Our body can be dissected and studied with our eyes, but when MIRs were invented, we could take pictures of what happens inside our brain as we think. MRI technology, quantum holographic technology, and satellites began to take pictures from space.

We, as average people, don't really understand what the government and large companies are doing in labs with million-dollar breaking-edge technology. Mainly because it's boring to many of us. It's not as fun as watching the Kardashians on TV. It's not as sexy as the Victoria Secret models in commercials.

It's not as cool as the Marvel movies or the shows we watch to entertain us.

A movie *Gemini* with Will Smith came out recently. The movie was about cloning an identical character to Will Smith's character. This technology may be available closer than we think—and maybe five years before it's mastered. Many other sci-fi shows, including *Living with Yourself* on Netflix, deal with cloning.

The future is here today. Tomorrow or in five years when someone reads these words it will have taken affect full force. I predict babies will be genetically modified to be cured for HIV. People will be born with increased defenses in their DNA based on the CRISPR DNA that has been found in bacteria. We'll be able to rewrite the code of life inside everything. Jelly fish genes will enable us to create a glow-in-the-dark dog. It has been done on other animals already. Mice have been created to fight lime disease. Mosquitos are being designed to fight Malaria. This world is on the brink of creating technology that addresses the questions about consciousness that will make our world shift. Science and religion are merging in many new and wonderful ways. This world is ripe for this merger. Our children's children will grow up in a world where they or their friends will have been affected physically by science.

IS SOMEONE LISTENING?

10/30/19 AMAZON PRIME AIRED A show by an astronaut who had a spiritual experience/awakening while looking at the earth from space. The way he described his experience is much the same as my experience. He said the feeling came from within. It was a feeling of gratitude trickling out all over his body. It was a pleasant feeling of lust, like during sex, or when you're in the middle of a great conversation.

He said we are all grieving a loss together—a vibration that is felt within the body—yet it seems to encompass the body as well. It is conscious and yet physical, like pressure on the skin and beyond the skin. Areas around the heart and muscles activate, and breath circulates life to areas the mind is connected to. The mind is a tool that we develop, and it needs to be programmed much the same way a baby needs to be programmed into the 3D world. It's the same way a new puppy needs to be house trained and taught words like sit. Feelings are extremely powerful.

Computers are smart. Internet advertisements are much like the quantum world, and the programing behind Facebook and other social media advertisements. Netflix and Amazon can even recommend shows to watch. They base their data from what you clicked on and what you like. Don't kid yourself. Sometimes your computers/smartphones/tv programs know you, so if this is the case, take a second to pay attention to the ads that come up on your Google home page or the YouTube videos on the right side of your screen.

Now realize something a little creepier. Each one of our smart phones also has a microphone and a camera on it. Most of us use the cloud and computers to back up our lives. So, smart people who have money want your money. They know you are going to shop and spend 65% of your income, and they know that 20% of your income is spent on entertainment. What you search will be used by their programming techniques to recommend ads for companies that pay them to do so. Part of the rat race is the cyber world we have created with technological advances. Money makes this modern world go around.

About 7 am the other morning, my wife and I randomly decided to run a marathon together. I didn't search online for any marathons coming up—it was just a casual conversation between us. But by 3 pm that same day I was on my Facebook scrolling down my news feed. And there it was. An ad for the Phoenix Rock and Roll Marathon coming up in a few weeks. I froze when I saw it. I put down my phone and I asked my wife if she searched online for a race or signed us up for one already. She said no. She hadn't thought about it again. So how did Facebook know to put that ad on my feed?

Here's another example. Over the last couple months I have been writing a book. Now my Facebook and other social media platforms have ads about self-publishing books. There are video links of people who are trying to help me sell the book better. My ads have changed simply because of what I'm doing on my computer. My behaviors have changed online. Shows I watch on Netflix have changed. The programs that Netflix recommends for me are all documentaries from the world of science. Take this to the quantum level here for a moment.

RESONATION

WE USE THIS WORD TO acknowledge an understanding of what someone is saying.

"Oh, I resonate with that."

"I agree with the concept and theory of what you are saying."

When we resonate with someone, we are on the same wavelength, and our energies are in sync on a deeper level. We naturally pick up what they mean when we talk with them. This is done instantly and without real effort. It's done by listening and focusing your imagination and attention on the person's words and actions. A connection is made with them on a quantum energy level that we are just now starting to realize with the new technologies available. In the near future, maybe in 5-10 years, it will be a known fact, and public schools will be teaching this quantum science in physics class. The science of epigenetic (the study of changes in organisms caused by modification of gene expression) will be taught in biology classes, anatomy classes, psychology classes or in the seminary.

CONNECTION TO MORE

THE CONNECTION I HAVE WITH the heartbeat of the Earth is undeniable now. At first, I thought it was all in my head, but now that it has happened, not just in my dreams but in my waking moments, I'm convinced. As I am writing now, the heartbeat feels strong. It's loud and yet gentle. It's in sync with me, present with me and with each breath that I take. I am placing my attention on the inside of me to sense the heart rhythm and pressure. I can also speed it up and feel it rush around.

That is why I stopped using caffeine. My heart seemed to beat chaotically when I was on caffeine—like I was having an anxiety attack. The extra energy was there, yes, but my body didn't know how to use it. When I was using the extra energy to run, ride my bike, or participate in a triathlon event, it was fine. But when I sat in a classroom or behind a computer, it didn't have an outlet. My body shook and the extra energy burned through me, zapping my energy along with giving me the feeling of being more tired than when I was active.

This threw me into stress, panic mode and a go-go-go mentality. It's much better for me to stay away from caffeine. I am already amped up most of the time. How does your body respond to caffeine?

WE ARE MORE

It takes a bigger person
to see beauty instead of ugly.
It takes a unique perspective
to analyze and recognize
the truth behind the lies.
There are many ways to the mountaintop.
There are many ways to live your life.
There may be many lifetimes
we all get to experience.
Our individual awareness
of who we are and why we are here
is not individually unique.
Humanity as a whole
is more connected than I ever knew.

As I evolve and as I progress in life
physically, mentally and spiritually,
I see the value in unity.
I see the value in erasing the lines
in the sand that we use to separate ourselves.
I also see the need to have them look
more like a staircase.
I see the need to break down barriers created in others.
I see that I am just a speck of dust
made up of the same energy
that is in all things.
The same dust and energy
that is in everything.
I am aware that I am more than I can imagine and
I want to help others
find their own connection to "more."

THE 3-D WORLD

10/31/19 WE LIVE IN A 3-D planet where we are on top of the world one moment and the next morning we are lost in the new day. We live in a world where we feel great and have a firm grasp of who we are and then that is shaken by fear or self-doubt. We live in a state of duality or positive/negative or yin/yang or sunrise/sunset. Why is that?

Some days I feel tremendous potential, where I can to do amazing things, and I'm grateful that I have the opportunity to be alive and to learn and grow. And then like this morning, I wake up feeling sluggish, tired, unmotivated, dreamy. I can't get going. It's almost like I am trying to hold onto the feeling I had the day before, not recognizing that it is a new day, and I have to reconnect all over again with the new moments this new day brings.

Money could be the equalizer in the game. No matter how we feel each day, money in the bank comes and goes. We have a limited amount of money to spend. Then we must make more, and sometimes we feel enslaved by it for taking up so many hours of each day.

Yes, we all need money to survive, and I ask myself how much money do I need to survive comfortably to take care of my three children, to help out my family when they need a little extra help, to be able to donate to charities? How many vacations do I want to take, and what is it going to cost? How much do I need for entertainment, cars, my kids' education? How much money is enough? We tend to throw our hands up and say, "I just need money." People who understand the rules of the financial game are better able to make a more educated decision based on the rules associated with money. If you don't, get a financial professional to help you.

YOUNG IMAGINATION

As a young kid my imagination ran wild—so much so that I had a hard time telling the truth when talking. I couldn't distinguish if something in my mind was real or not. I didn't know if what I saw on TV or read or learned about in school was any different than the information I imagined in my head.

I remember walking with Jeremy one day in 2nd grade. I started to tell him about owls and how cool they were. I made up a story about them and how I saw one and how I know all about them. I remember the story because I knew I was making it all up, but I couldn't stop. He kept asking how I knew about owls and I said, "I just do." But that question stuck in my mind. I wondered why I presented all that information as fact instead of telling him it was from my imagination.

I struggled with this story for many years. In fact, while reading the book *The Four Agreements* (One of the agreements is to be impeccable with your word) and Dean Radin's book, *Real Magic*, I realized our words were magic. Words are a big part of communication, and yet there is so much more: facial expressions, pitch and hand gestures, laughter, telepathic communication, vibes or energy. Music communicates a vibration that we are drawn to as well. Hearing brings a heightened sense that enables us to feel how it resonates.

Often, I forget to do one simple exercise that could save me a lot of heartache. It's projecting my imagination into the future. It's taking the fork in the road with my powerful imagination and sitting back and asking myself how do I feel? Three minutes after making the power leap through time into the future I ask how does this feel? What obstacles do I not foresee? Can I take this one hour into the future? Can I foresee the next several major roadblocks and interactions that will challenge me? Are those challenges going to change the path I'm on and take me to a different one? Was the other fork in the road a better path to align me with my highest and best purpose?

The conscious mind is a powerful tool that can help determine memories, thoughts and feelings we've had in the past. It is a wonderful tool we can use. Even more is available to do this. Imagination draws from more than just the brain. It draws from the brain of the stomach. It draws from the vibrations of the skin. It draws from the powerful heartbeat of the earth, and the breath of the air around us. It links us to the knowing we have when the hairs on the back of our necks stands up.

This power is within all of us. We have more resources to draw from than we are using now. It's happening *within* whether you are aware of it or not. The more time you spend developing this ability, the stronger it gets. Funny how that works. The more you read, study and dive into a subject, the more you learn. The more you exercise your body, the stronger it gets. The more you focus on the *now,* and live in the moment, the quieter the background noise gets. Whatever you consciously direct your energy toward is the path.

When I think about my time with my good friend Tanner, I know that we shared in the light and love of conversation until I got a horrible feeling in my chest. It was overwhelmingly powerful and sad. The feeling came about on a subject that is dark for me. This subject—heaven and hell—has been bottled up inside me for a long time, so it hurts. I had hoped to be non-biased in my view of it, yet religion draws a line in the sand with this subject.

People are either on the left or the right side of the line, and the subject has brought much pain to people over the centuries. Wars have been fought and families have been divided. Severe consequences have come to those who didn't obey the rules because "good" people knew what was right. These good people feel so strongly that their path was the one and only true path—their mission in life—they don't accept those who don't see the truth as they do.

Since I have not died and gone to the other side, I am not an expert. I do have my own ever-changing beliefs about God, heaven and hell, energy, good vs. evil, right and wrong. But the one thing I can say with complete certainty is that the Light is unconditional love. The power and force of true energy is love.

Love is for all things.
Love has an unconditional
way of not judging.
Love doesn't draw lines in the sand and
force people to be on either side.
Love doesn't divide.
It unifies.
It overcomes.
It is patient and allows others
to make mistakes.
It allows others to live and enjoy and experience life
in their own unique way.
This doesn't mean love is a push-over.
Love is hard.
It is firm, yet it flows like water.
It is adaptable.
Yet it can be a wave
that smashes against the rock
turning stone into sand.

POWER WITHIN US

WE HAVE POWER WITHIN US to know the truth, and it is waiting on us to be aware of it. It is waiting for us to put down the phone, get off the computer, stop wasting time at the bar, and focus on being aware of the journey.

Focus on the energy around you.
Focus on the life you were meant to live.
Focus on the obstacles in your way.
Focus on the strengths you have
to overcome those obstacles.
Focus on the next layer of life.
Focus on the game
you are caught up in.
Be aware of the key players and
the energy they put off.
See the world
for what it truly is.

Truth is in the eye of the beholder. Don't lie to yourself and don't allow lies to come out of your mouth. Don't fool yourself into lying at all. Don't mislead yourself, because if you do, you will bring confusion. You will be swallowed up by the lies you have told about yourself. You will put energy into the lies, and they will become real. Your imagination will make it so. Instead of lying to yourself, focus on truth. What do you know that is true?

The life some people live is called heaven on earth. But be warned. Be careful what you wish for! You have the power to get it, so be careful what truth you find. Wants, hidden fantasies, desires and first thoughts seem like truths, but they are, in fact, illusions that we tell ourselves as protection as we evolve. Be cautious in this approach. Do the work necessary to find the real truth within. Your own truth. Not what you've heard or read or seen—what you know deep down inside.

FIND YOURSELF

HOW DO YOU FIND YOURSELF? We all know that it takes trial and error; it takes pain to make the good worth having. It takes a battle to conquer life. In Sue Morter's book, *The Energy Codes,* she has created exercises that allow your inner struggle to happen. These exercises allow our imagination and conscious/subconscious mind to sync. She has amazing breathing techniques and yoga practices that align with chakras and energy blocks to help the soulful self emerge. I have been doing this work for some time now and have turned off my autopilot mode. The world has opened and responded in kind. The old saying, "You reap what you sow," is true. The power of our thoughts is beyond our realization.

TOOLS

HYPOCRISY IS PART OF LIFE. If you are human, you have been a hypocrite at one point or another in your life. Let's realize something important here. My thoughts are like a wave and I follow them. It is up to me to organize my thoughts and write them in a way that you, the reader, can understand. I am like a scientist analyzing my thoughts to get a good baseline to look back on as I progress. Journaling is a great way to begin. This might be true for you too. What I have discovered is that the life we live is the greatest tool we have to evaluate ourselves. People in your life are here to help you in some way, but you might not be able to understand that when you are focused on 3D problems—like how to pay the bills.

The farther you dive away from your centered mind, the more incoherent you are. Your heart beats and your rhythms are being forced. The more you start to wake up, you realize that you are not aware—and being not aware is a good thing. Trust me it won't feel like a good thing when it comes, though. It will not feel normal. Because to this point, it hasn't been your normal. Or maybe you have experienced what I am talking about, but you just lost the discipline to stay with it because it was too hard. That's okay too.

Remember the old saying that tells us we must "Rest in God." Well, there is so much truth in this simple statement that has shaped religion. The greatest commandments are: 1) know thy God—or whatever name you use, and 2) love thy neighbor. The Golden Rule tells us to treat others as we want to be treated. Life has a set of rules, yet it's based on free will. We are free to do what we want—but we are not free from the consequences of what we do.

Our world has been designed
by powers greater than us.
The world is perfect the way it is.
It is designed with choices and consequences.
With evil and good.
With the poor and rich.
Famous people and hermits.
Royal families and simple families.
Some have fewer choices than others,
but we do have choices.
Every moment.
It could be as simple as
focusing our awareness,
imagination
and energy
into this now moment.
We have choices.

Many wonderful songs have been written about this subject. Many religions have been formed to help guide us from the mistakes that will mislead us. However, the game is an individual one. How does family play into that role? My father summed up responsibility for me pretty well the other day. He said, "If you want an easy life, you shouldn't have had a family." However, I love my kids and I wouldn't trade any of them or the experiences I have had. Why not? Well, they are all a blessing to me. They have all shown me wonderful things that I would never have discovered if they hadn't been born! All I know is that the challenges of this life are meant to be overcome. This is not anything new here; I am simply connecting the dots and putting the puzzle pieces together from what I have observed.

The back and forth throughout my thoughts are constant. Repairing my family is among the top priorities I have. Making peace with those I have wronged or hurt in my own mind is important. Following up on the commitments I have made is important. Living life in a way that I unify my own life is the goal. It should be your goal as well.

The grass isn't always greener on the other side, but then again how would you know if you are not brave enough to explore it? Life and time are not the simple equations we once thought. This life and the evolutions and the world we live in are designed for growth. We are in a habitat that points to this everywhere we turn. So, by looking around, you will be aware of the truth of this statement. What you do about it is up to you!

MEDITATION

Let's do a meditation together. Take a few minutes and breathe in and out. Slow down and sink into yourself for a minute. Allow whatever you had on your mind to float away. Breathe in. Feel your heartbeat slow down. Hold your breath for five seconds, and feel the control as you hold your breath. Exhale while in control and feel your lungs. Push the air out. Hold your breath again for five seconds. Feel the control you have. Now allow your breath to be natural. What does this natural breath feel like to you?

Relax your mind. Your conscious mind can control your breath, but it doesn't have to. Your subconscious mind is stronger and knows what to do. Relax into your body. Your body also knows what to do and you will breathe naturally. Let go of your conscious mind and allow it to relax. Allow your conscious mind to be an observer to the breath. Allow it to feel the inflation of your lungs as they breathe in. Focus your mind on your lungs as you breathe. Feel with your mind the stretch within your lungs one inch at a time. Allow yourself to feel the muscles tighten around your lungs. Force the air out. Allow your mind to relax and let your breath take over. (PAUSE)

Think of those who you love and those who love you. Allow

yourself to sink into the feeling of love. The true heartbeat and rhythm within. The power and strength of unconditional love a parent has for a child. Or an innocent child has for a loving parent. (PAUSE)

Take a few moments, and then when you are ready, open your eyes and come back to the present moment.

In meditation, we can allow the journey to progress as it is meant to progress. We all have evolved to this point in time, with our own memories and experiences that make us aware of whatever truths we hold dear. No matter who you are, life has brought you experiences.

Meditation is a freeing experience for anger, pain and love. After meditating, I showed my family the love I felt coursing through me, and somehow, I was cleansed. I still had some pain in my elbow, but a new awareness took its place with the light feeling of love. I accepted myself, and I had the ability to say yes, I am human, I am not perfect. And that's ok.

EXPLORE TO HEAL

BE AWARE OF YOUR THOUGHTS, how they feel, and choose to spread more love around you. This is truly a gift—the self knows the answers. This connection knows the answers. How might we tap into them and discover them you ask? First become aware and then bring that awareness into each moment.

Breathe in the future and
exhale the past.
Be the creator of your life and
know that you are the one
who is behind your eyes.
You are the one reading this message.
You are the one who is looking for answers.
You are the one who is answering them.
This life has many hidden mysteries.
If you look under the illusion
and see truth,
you will know.

How you get there again is step one. Become aware of your thoughts. Look at your past actions. Think back on the memories and hurtful pain you have hidden away. But instead of focusing on the pain, ask what were you meant to learn from those experiences? Can you bring each one to light and see the other emotions and feelings buried inside of you? What are they? Are there beautiful messages hidden away like the box I had hidden away with my father? How deep can you go?

How much pain has this already caused in your life? Isn't it easier to try something new? Have you had enough karma and pain over this yet? Did you create these circumstances in your life to help you learn something? What would that be? What can you possibly be trying to teach yourself with pain, suffering, love, passion?

How can we have good without evil? Is this world perfect the way it is? Do we have to have the freedom of choice to choose because without it we wouldn't evolve? Once we become aware, then what? Is there more? We will find out as life goes on. What should we do in this moment to help make sure we are aware of what is happening? We can choose the best path.

Imagination is a wonderful gift. We need to have the creativity and power to look within ourselves and identify our memories as a blessing. Ones that can be used for good or bad, or for choices and consequences. You can use your imagination to say to yourself *If I choose option A, I will continue to shut these feeling down, or box up these thoughts and emotions. I can keep going with life as it is now and that's okay. I will pick this up later when I am ready to deal with it. It's okay I trust in myself, to know when the time is right.* Think on this and carry this vision for a couple of minutes, and sit with the next couple of major moments that this might bring up.

Use your imagination to determine what you want. Does this create the life you want to live? Does this give energy to the direction and path you want to follow? Is this for your highest and best purpose? If the answer is yes, you are not ready to bottle it up. If it is no, and you are ready for a change, you want to become aware of other choices. Then ask the same questions and answer them with your imagination for the B path. Is this what you want? If so, pursue it. Follow this line of questioning as often as time permits. If you practice this exercise, the process will take much less time. Do it regularly.

Start to feel the energy around you differently. Start to be aware of the love people share for you and the love you share for others. See that it is not as important to get that promotion, or that you get rich or have the fanciest car, or simply the illusion of the lifestyle you want. Let down your mask. Let the light in. Open the boxes you have hidden deep within you and the emotions that are associated with them.

Eventually you will see that there is a light under the cloud. You will see that there is love under the locked feelings and energy blocks. Eventually you will see that the possibility of life itself is a gift. "It's a gift to us from us for us," as Dr. Sue would say. "You'll see that the house rules are real," as Dan Millman would say. The door within us is a corner few of us have yet to turn. Find the strength and will power necessary to bring back the magic. Find the gifts you possess and the strength you have to share your inner beauty with those around you. Think of the love you can share. How good can you get it?

Spirituality is a part of daily life. It is in the interactions we have with our kids. It's in the interactions we have with strangers around us. It's the light that others show us that dissolves the energy blocks and allows love to wash through us. It's simply the golden rule: Treating others as you want to be treated.

Today's new age is a world full of information. Information is abundant, so I encourage you to find the book, teacher, mentor, video, TED talk, blog, movie, person, religion, audio tape, school, or job that matches with how you learn best. Find what matches with your experiences in each subject and develop your own view. Develop your own awareness. Develop your own creative genius within and unlock the secrets this world has to offer you.

Chapter 6

BEHIND THE DARK CLOUD

Journal

SPECIAL LIFE

My relationship with my father is special.
The time it took to heal our relationship is special.
The moment of forgiveness is special.
My relationship now with my father is
deeper and more genuine
than ever before.
What changed?
The feelings and memories I
brought to light and
the strength that I found
to recognize our different perspectives
are key.
The only way I was able to do that
was through a miracle.
A miracle that healed
the blocked energy
from within
my own heart.

Despite this darkness I have lived with for so long, I have had so many beautiful moments in my life. Don't think that because I am sharing the pain, there wasn't the same amount of joy and love. My children and the life they have are proof of that. Yes, I created turmoil and destruction as I walked through life, but I didn't mean to. I am trying my best to figure out myself and at the same time limit the damage done to others.

A NEW PERSPECTIVE

6-28-2019 I COULD SEE HOW being open to other ideas would have been better. I have so many built-up issues and memories with my father that I eventually had to limit them or put them into a box. I took that box and buried it deep inside me, never to let out my anger, hurt, frustration, confusion, hate, deep dark pain or it would ruin everything.

Over the years, when the subject in that box was approached— like when someone would say, "You're stupid like your father." I would link the word father to my deeply hidden memory box, and memories associated with my feelings I didn't want to come up, did come up. The box of father-feelings was released. They snuck out of the memory box like a black cloud slipping out of fresh cracks.

These dark clouds spilled into my mind and I breathed them in. I inhaled the feelings deep into my lungs and I breathed the cloud out again. It came out in feelings of anger, sadness and hurt, with deep dark pain coming to the surface, spreading into the present.

But my reality was shifting, and I could no longer control it. As I breathed more of this cloud, it spread with every exhaled breath. I breathed in the past, and during the quiet moments of being present, between breaths, I created my reality. The feelings changed. I began to breathe in new feelings and exhaled the past and stepped into the reality of today. I realized that I was hurt. I had pain. Father hurt and confused me. Knowing that, I had a choice to make. The choice was to be aware of how I was feeling, or try to shove it back down again, like I always did. This time I was more aware of my feelings.

Maybe I am aware of them because I am in the space where I can look at different perspectives and see a different angle now. I have two sons and a daughter of my own. I am responsible for them, much the same way my father was for me. I do the best that I can for them at this present time. I am no hero. I am no savior to them. I am barely on their radar sometimes. Just now, they are thinking of me and developing their mind like I did back then, as I looked at my father. Each one of them sees me in a different way. It's just like how my brothers and sisters see our father differently than I do. In fact, my little brother, years younger than me, said Dad was different in almost every aspect. What was the change?

The obvious answer is time. But also, other things truly did change between my father and myself. Both of us had anger coming from the box, but love was also buried deep under our painful emotions. Did my father also show me love along with the hurtful, painful memories? Is there a gray area in between these thoughts? If so, what are they? Where are they? Oh, I see. They were under this locked cloud inside a dark corner, inside a sealed-off basement room under the door, with a "Do Not Open" sign, under the volcano of doom, on top of the mound of years of shoving bottled-up energy.

It took a lot of work and energy to shut them up—into locking away this cloud of hurt and pain and over-sensitivity to the awareness. I still have confusing and deep issues with my father to work out. So better to shove those aside until a time I can pull them up and deal with them.

Yes, that was exactly what happened. Until now! Why now? What has changed to make me aware of this now? It seems strange that this is coming out. Let me record it. Let me examine this feeling of why. Let me talk into my phone for almost 40 minutes and then send this recording to my brother Joey and my wife Flavia and then eventually to my father. Why?

The energy I felt coming out of this box wasn't just pain anymore. I let the pain in, and I breathed it out. I looked it up and down to reevaluated it. The energy was no longer dark—there were beautiful lights of love inside. There were strong feelings of love, happiness, joy, creativity, gratefulness, and peace inside. Oh my God! What was under that cloud literally changed as I breathed it out.

It literally turned into a feeling of strength, power, love, confidence and pure joy that I can only describe as blissful—a heaven on earth. Breathing in the new feelings and energies underneath the cloud of LOVE from a father to a son and love from a son to a father. Love from a daughter to a father. Love from a father to a daughter. Father from my father to my grandfather. The sad death and tragedy of my grandfather and its impact on my father, and how it hurt him. How he was hurt in many ways by his parents that I am now blaming him for in my life.

My father came from someplace.
Growing up,
he learned things
just as I did.
He is human.
We are all here to learn and
grow and awaken within ourselves.
This love feeling is deep and
powerful and can be the answer!
It can heal this pain and
turn this locked
imagination-created vault aside.

Questions like these come up and the answers to them come from a place I haven't fully discovered or was not evolved enough to see. Maybe in the next years of my life, I will have the ability to look back at today and think similar thoughts as these to help me redirect my energy. I spent all those years in vain. I incorrectly followed the wrong path. Maybe a healing path with more true, unconditional love like that of God's love. That of a father to a son can heal. Maybe the depth of this view of God and father have yet to be discovered. Maybe it is okay that we are on a journey to find out. So, buckle up. Let's enjoy the ride. I am curious to see what happens next and what we can discover from it.

MY CHILDREN

THIS BRINGS ME TO MY love for my children. **Ethan** was born in 2004. I learned to love more when I had the opportunity to meet my first-born baby boy Ethan. Ethan, you came into my life at a young age. I was 19, just barely getting out of high school.

I can remember, as if it were yesterday, the summers I spent outside working at your age. The hard life lessons I learned much the same way you are now learning. You recently spent a week working with my dad and my brother. You had the same opportunities to learn the value of hard work I did. Oh, wait…is that a true statement? Did you learn the value of hard work like I did growing up? No, not at all. You didn't have the same life I had when I grew up. For one thing, you bounce back and forth between two families. You have two houses and two mothers, and you have been doing this since you were two years old.

I feel I have wronged you in many ways, Ethan. I know this and I am sorry. In many ways, I have given you a harder life than I had because I didn't provide you stability. You grew up with four parents. You grew up with half-brothers and sisters. You grew up in two houses, miles apart. I can't imagine what that was like. I didn't grow up the same way. So how can I possibly imagine you getting the same lessons from life. Could it be that my imagination is limited to the experiences I have had in life? Yes, it is.

Today you are fifteen years old and constantly reminding me how life changes. I see too much of myself in you. Currently you are facing some of the hardest years of your young life, and I want you to know I love you with all my heart. You could never do anything that would lessen that love. Sure, at times I may be hard on you. But that's because I am responsible for you.

"Stop, it's hammer time now!" "Stop, in the name of LOVE." Stop in the name of yourself with the big second part of unconditional love attached. You know the kind that allows things to happen in their due course. The patient kind of love that will sit back for years as your own kids make wrong choices, until years later when your kids see the struggle you had—just with different eyes.

We are each different people throughout this one life. I am hoping by letting my mask fall away, I will enjoy more of your life and more of my life. I will find peace, and not just work 40 hours a week. I will take more time to spend with the ones I love, to develop in the areas of life I want to focus on, and to evolve. We all make daily sacrifices to support you kids growing up while being true to what we identify as love. I intend to expand the layers in my own hard head.

Oh boy, those who know me know I am stubborn and stuck in my ways when I get something in my head. And those who have known me longer will see that when I am finally able to recognize how wrong I have been, on so many issues, I am grateful to those who have given me the patience to evolve. They gave me the time to pursue life my way and the unconditional love. I didn't see until later—sometimes when it was too late. I am sorry. I am sorry I have hurt you. I am sorry that in the past, I couldn't reciprocate that unconditional love. We do have today and tomorrow to make it better.

Ryan was born in 2010. Ryan is my youngest son and I was in a much different place in life when he was born. I was 26 years old with many more life experiences. Some of them hardened me, but like the stone tossed around by the ocean waves, my rough edges were smoothed over and I learned to adapt to life.

I learned to make money. I learned the value of credit. I learned the value of education. I took online classes at night through University of Phoenix. I had friends who came over and hung out. We had a social life that was mellow. Nothing too crazy, just a very mellow, ordinary life. It seemed that I learned to center myself and my family against the storm. Yes, we still struggled. Yes, I still went through the economic crash of 2008.

Losing my new house, my job, Jessica's mother. Losing my best friend Shaun. Losing things outside of myself during these years. It was hard. Very hard! However, I had an autopilot mode I could return to. I had the defenses in place already and I knew how to compartmentalize well now. I knew how to bottle up and swallow my own personal issues. Or at least I thought I did.

I am happy to say that I didn't lose Ryan's mother, even though our marriage ended badly. I have a lot of guilt inside for the way things ended. She and I are co-parents now. Ryan, my beautiful blonde blue-eyed baby boy has my heart. He is special to us and everyone else who meets him. I have the privilege to be in his life.

I know my son! I love him with every ounce of my being. Because of this love, I am still trying to get ahold of the demons buried within. I want to be a good father to him and all my kids. I want to be stronger for them. Often times I have not been strong. I am, in fact, very torn inside. I have a lot of hurt and pain and sadness bottled up from everyday ordinary life events.

As I write these words I am in tears. I can barely see what it is I am writing. The flood of emotions going through me right now is overpowering. I want to release them. I have been holding on to the pain and frustration and guilt and shame for too long. I need them to heal. By writing this down and taking a hard look in the mirror, I hope to allow some of this blocked energy to heal. I hope to allow the beauty to come out from the darkness that overpowers the light.

Ryan, I want you to know that I love you also with all my heart! You are the second oldest son—just like me when I was born. Only you don't have a stronger older sister to kick your butt when you are acting funny in school like I did. Your older brother is seven years older than you and not in the same school. However, you have the ability to watch and learn from his mistakes and his accomplishments. You both do! You both have lived a very similar life, and you and Ethan are brothers! You are my sons. You are both worthy of all of it. You are worthy and you deserve the best in life. Be careful though. Be warned. Because you are worthy and because you can achieve your hearts' desire.

Julia was born in 2016. Julia knows me as Daddy. She knows me as her daddy. She sees me with the innocence only children can have. She looks past my flaws and pain and sees the real me. She touches the parts of me that I hope to become. She makes me feel worthy and alive. I want to stop time and allow the moments to last forever. I want to protect her from the pain within. I don't ever want her to stop seeing me as Daddy.

The times spent with you have changed me into a better man. The times I tucked you in at night left me walking away with watery eyes—full of love and gratitude. The hours spent playing and talking have reminded me what it is like to be a child. I remember spending hours alone on the couch or in my room using my imagination much the same way you do. I hope you can keep that imagination flowing. When I was your age, they didn't really allow children to express themselves like we have allowed you to do. You have that choice. Everyone is more accepting of what some call New Age beliefs. But you will still have to find out who you are. You will still be tried in a thousand different ways in life. Your obstacles might hurt you, but never break you. They will be steppingstones to a higher view.

I have no doubt you will grow up to be a beautiful, marvelous, intelligent, unique, relentlessly determined Julia! I also want you to know that I love you. You are also a part of me. I am part of you! We all are worthy of unconditional love. We all will make mistakes but just like the kitchen wall in our house says: "In this house…we are real. We *make* mistakes. We say I'm sorry. We give second chances. We have fun. We give hugs. We forgive. We do really loud. We are patient. We love."

FLAVIA

THE AGE OLD SAYING THAT behind every good man is a great woman is true in my case. However, some would argue the fact that I am not a good man. No one could argue the fact that I have a rock-solid ride or die partner in Flavia. I have put her through a lot over the years. I have tested the strength of our relationship time and time again—just as the storm rolls in at night and the wild winds destroy everything in its path. The sun still rises on a new day. Flavia is the sun rising in my life. She is my constant despite the storm. Together we have learned to adapt and overcome the obstacles thrown in our way. We have learned the value of honest communication. No one is perfect. We all make mistakes, but we are forever and always.

Flavia is the one I love. She allows me to be myself. She is standing in my corner cheering me on, even as I stumble my way through this journey. Our partnership is always adapting and changing as all things do. Our relationship isn't a perfect one full of fictional story book endings. We have our rough edges as all relationships do. However, Flavia is my true friend.

I am a lone wolf who has found love.
Who has connected with another.
This connection makes me feel
part of the pack.
Flavia is the key to this connection.
She is the head of the pack.
Forcing me to learn and
evolve out of my caveman ways.
Helping me to pick my head up and
strive to be a better man.
Softening my rough spots and
connecting me closer to the
gentle, kinder side within.
Holding my hand as we face
some of the obstacles we created.
Kissing my check softly and
telling me it's okay in the night.
Knowing that she has my back and
is my forever and always strengthens me.
It helps me to sit up straighter and
posture up with pride.
Without her laugh to fill the air
I would have been lost at sea.
Without her love to bind us all together
we would be missing
a crucial piece of the puzzle.

8/26/19 Flavia, as my wife is very hard on me. She has challenged me and made me question why I do things. Through this battle I have struggled many times with many different issues. She's mainly asking me to talk her love language and be present with her. It is hard for me to do when I am coming back to myself with all the issues. But that is simply the point. She is asking me to focus my attention and engage. She is wanting me to speak to her and communicate and create a life with her. She wants me to pay attention when she talks. She wants to actually have me around. She isn't satisfied with just the small amount of leftover attention I have for her.

I am forced to fight my demons, to raise up and overcome the challenges I face. It is a blessing in disguise. One that forced me to the point of frustration again. I would leave and not give the love that I felt she already had. But the reality is, I haven't been myself and she knows it. I haven't been doing my best and she sees it. She sees the opportunities I let slip by. She sees the lack of effort I have had and energy I have had to handle simple normal everyday tasks.

She calls me out and forces me to question why I am doing a certain thing. She is my half that is better at communicating. She is so different than anyone I have ever known. She calls me out on all my BS. Therefore, she is helping me see more in myself. It is her questioning and ability to stick by my side while I struggle inside that shows me the power of love.

Why I am appreciative of such a strong woman? My ride and

die. My 50/50. My voice of reason. My rock. She has known my many sides. She has seen me at my best and my worst. She lets me be relaxed and be myself. Breathing in air isn't so bad around her. Someone who gets me.

She thinks I am too much at times, and she's right. I appreciate everything she puts up with. I know because of her pushing me to do better and be a better person, husband, father, employee, person who does what they say they will do—I am a better version of myself than I have ever been before. You are an angel who has played a huge role in my life.

8/31/19 I don't think I give enough credit to the people in my life who are the planners, like Flavia. They enable me to be free and just go with the flow. They take on the stress of handling the venues we go to. The food we eat. The transportation. They handle the details that enable the rest of us to relax and enjoy ourselves. Those people who plan, research, coordinate and communicate all the fun events are like unsung song we need to sing. We need to take a step back and say thank you and appreciate them for a moment. They keep the action alive. So thank you!

LIFE LONG LEARNING

8/6/19 THIS JOURNAL IS HOPEFULLY the final one for today. I was just watching the second show on Gaia.com/TV. I have witnessed two random shows that populated as I logged into my account on my TV to relax and enjoy. The shows that I watched were like a message hitting me now.

I have seen my favorite authors like Sue Morter doing specials with this TV Network. In fact, that's why I downloaded her book in the first place. It happened about a month after I subscribed and paid for a yearly membership. They had so many good YouTube videos that I knew I needed to subscribe.

The truth that I keep stumbling on is evidence of the power of my writing. The life-changing, dramatic, snowball effect happening in my life, at this very moment, is the truth of it. Me being able to simply sit down currently in my life and write these words has been healing. So much inside has shifted. The stars have aligned in such a way to allow me to express myself. I have said yes to those stars. My guides, the voices inside, the angel and the devil on my shoulder, my soulful self, whatever you call it. Whatever the connection to the energy I am talking about in this book.

That's it!

MY HOPE

8/8/19 I hope all my entries from this point forward are going in the right direction. I hope I found a new ability and awareness that will allow me to stop, slow down, and just be grateful that I am alive and breathing and experiencing my life. As Dan Millman puts it, "How good can I get it!"

Can I open the kundalini energy within that yoga and meditations masters spend a lifetime opening? Maybe that shift has already happened. Maybe that new energy is flowing into my chakras now and expanding my awareness. Maybe my energy is shifting, and I am evolving into a higher energy frequency. Maybe I am just losing my mind and am going crazy being stupid happy, and maybe this bubble will burst.

I guess there is only one way to find out. Time! It has been said that time is the great equalizer. But today, now, my imagination has opened. It is dancing for joy in all the small but marvelous, miraculous moments unfolding around me that I am lucky enough to be aware of in a new light. I can't lie to myself and say this new feeling will be the end-all cure-all. But I can say that I can see a successful life created by my own internal power start to emerge. Yes, that might sound glum. But to those who are in the darkest part of the storm, know that there is a light. If you endure and you allow yourself to stop rushing around in panic overdrive mode, this might be a fortune cookie that says, "Stop and smell the roses."

My advice is to journal your moments. Study them, meditate on them, do yoga with them in mind, focus on the connection they have to your actions. Discuss them with your closest friends. Bring awareness and light to every hidden corner within. Your actions will identify and bring awareness to how your energy is spent.

If your life is great and you don't have any problems, you are a God! However, if your life sucks and you are thinking *I can't do this anymore, I am going to kill myself or others, if I can't figure this out*, well, you are also a GOD! We all are! God is within just as much as he is without. Whatever you call GOD it is correct. But remember, you don't have all the answers. You haven't truly experienced the reality of the future. You have a partial piece of the picture and it is limited. Don't draw a line in the sand. Don't push down and block out other perspectives because of your limited view.

God is said to have unconditional love.
God is said to be able to heal all things.
God is said to have a plan in place for this life.
God is said to be able to bring light to the darkness.
God is said to allow free will to reign.
What God is said to have
is real with no limited view.
I believe that what most call GOD
is bigger than my limited mind can understand.
I don't want to draw lines in the sand
when I don't fully comprehend
the vast subjects of the universe.

Love surpasses all. Together we must allow the power of love to shine its light on our confusion. We must do the work necessary to allow love to dissolve the illusions around us. It is vital to our success in this new world. It always has been and always will be the correct path to take.

It is the only way to slow down and allow ourselves the freedom of choice that was intended. The freedom to act. The freedom to live. The freedom to evolve. The freedom to be our authentic selves, flowing like water into the stream of life.

To expand our focus large enough to see the layers within, we must slow down. Breathe in the future and breathe out the past. Allow the energy to flow. See more by becoming aware of more than just your bully or your anger. Don't associated with feelings of anger. See more. Be more. Do more. Allow your internal battles to lead to correct actions that align with your highest and best purpose.

Be loving.
Whatever that means to you.
We must do the work necessary
to feel the will within.
Growth will create
the life we are meant to experience.
The desire and willpower are within.
We are already creating our own reality.
We are just becoming aware of it.
We are creating an internal hell or
a heaven within!
Stop pretending we are not!
You are already creating and
experiencing each moment!
You have more control
of your inner self
than you can imagine.
Allow your imagination
to create what you will.

8/2/19 – It was fun while it lasted. The End! Now just do it! And Journal for yourself!

EPILOGUE

12/6/19 I WAS READING THE draft of this book and I realized something profound has been happening. I am more aware of my habits, patterns and actions. More specifically, when I said that I never really hurt people. Writing that was a way to release the energy and only hurt myself. And when I wrote those words, I was telling the truth—I didn't recall hurting anyone. However, since that time, I realize that wasn't quite accurate. I have hurt people.

The importance of being truthful starts with us. I have said many times that I follow the words of Gandhi and want to be the change I wish to see in this world. That means that I must be truthful and not downplay or lie to myself. Since this isn't confession time, I don't feel the need to explain all my wrong doings. This public format is not the place for me to unlock the pandora box of Andrew's wrongs in life.

Since the intention of writing this book is to document my awakening and evolution, and share it with people with the intent to help those who are struggling with life, I would like to focus on the lesson of forgiveness for a moment before I close this book.

We hurt the ones we love the most. Someone smarter than me once said that and I know this to be the truth. I have hurt the ones I have loved the most. I have wronged the people who have been the closest to me in life. As I go through the memories of the trauma and the pain I have caused with my behavior, I realize that I used part of my own energy to drown out the memories.

I blocked the pain I have caused. I ignored my actions that were destructive. I chalked it up to the substances I have abused over the years—alcohol, food, sex, or any device to help numb the memory of the damage I've created. This is a cycle that is hard to break.

It's much easier to deal with the pain other people have caused me. It's much easier to point the finger and blame them or come up with other reasons to justify my actions. The fact that I'm not the only one who does this is no comfort. One of the secrets and great mysteries of life is really very simple and it's always easier to say than to do: Truth will set us free.

We must regain our ability to control ourselves. We must forgive ourselves and let go of the blocked energy and heal the pain we have caused others. We must remember the consequences of our actions. We must remember, so that when we wake up tomorrow and life presents a similar pattern, we will act with the consequences in mind. We must choose to act with love, patience and kindness both for ourselves and for others.

We must learn from our own mistakes and we must do better.

When we fall, we must shorten the time it takes for us to forgive and learn. Today marks the moment I have witnessed my own faults. I have been brought to my knees as I have been shown the ripple effect of my actions. My choices have consequences. For the ones I have wronged in this life, I want you to know that I am truly sorry. Please forgive me.

In order to truly love myself, I must learn to forgive myself. This book has been a lesson in self-care that makes me extremely grateful. Although it has been a hard year of reflection to overcome many barriers and mistakes, I feel blessed that the stars have aligned to allow me to wake up.

Material things in life come and go. Even if I had all my wishes granted in this life, and had all the answers presented to me, the joy of having these answers would fade. The joy of having new toys would fade. At the end of the day, I will still be me. Therefore, I must learn to let go and accept the fact that I am enough. One day I hope to truly say those words and have them resonate with the echo of absolute truth.

BOOKS FOR THE JOURNEY

Many authors from around the world have helped me without ever knowing me personally. I want to thank the authors who have helped me overcome some of my life's obstacles, by being brave enough to share their stories. Below is a list of authors I recommend.

I haven't read all these books yet, but some of them I have read more than once. Some of them I have spent hours contemplating over the years. Some of them spoke inside my head after I made a mistake when I knew better. Maybe you'll find some of them beneficial for your journey through life.

Ted Andrews, *Sacred Sounds: Transformation through Music and Word*

Lisa Barnett, *From Questioning to Knowing: 73 Prayers to Transform Your Life*

Stephen Batchelor, *Buddhism Without Beliefs: A Contemporary Guide to Awakening*

Joseph Campbell, *Transformations of Myth Through Time*

Sonia Choquette, Ph.D., *The Psychic Pathway*

Frank Close, *The Infinity Puzzle: Quantum Field Theory and the Hunt for an Orderly Universe*

Paulo Coelho, *The Alchemist*

Joe Dispenza, *Becoming Supernatural: How Common People are Doing the Uncommon*

Dr. Wayne Dyer, *Mastering the Present Moment: Healing Wisdom*

John Edward, *Infinite Quest: Develop Your Psychic Intuition to Take Charge of your Life*

Danielle Egnew, *True Tales of the Truly Weird: Real Paranormal Accounts from a Real Psychic*

Richard Feynman, *QED: The Strange Theory of Light and Matter*

Amanda Gefter, *Trespassing on Einstein's Lawn: A Father, a Daughter, the Meaning of Nothing, and the Beginning of Everything*

Louisa Gilder, *The Age of Entanglement:When Quantum Physics Was Reborn*

Jonathan Goldman, *The 7 Secrets of Sound Healing*

Carl Greer, Ph.D. Psh.D, *Change Your Story, Change Your Life: Using Shamanic and Jungian Tools to Achieve Personal Transformation*

Pam Grout, *Nine Do-it-Yourself Energy Experiments that Prove Your Thoughts Create Your Reality*

Bhante Gunaratana, *Mindfulness in Plain English*

Carl A. Hammerschlag, M.D., *The Dancing Healers: A Doctor's Journey of Healing with Native Americans*

Thich Nhat Hanh, *The Miracle of Mindfulness: An Introduction to the Practice of Meditation* and *Making Space: Creating a Home Meditation Practice*

Dan Harris, *10% Happier: How I Tamed the Voice in My Head, Reduced Stress Without Losing My Edge, and Found Self-Help That Actually Works—A True Story*

Dr. Dain Heer, *Being You: Changing the World*

James Hillman, *The Soul's Code: In Search of Character and Calling*

Tammy J. Holmes, *Remembering One, Once Again: Twelve Principles that will Change Your Life*

Jon Kabat-Zinn, *Wherever You Go, There You Are* and *Mindfulness Meditation In Every Day Life*

David Kaise, *How Hippies Saved Physics: Science, Counterculture, and the Quantum Revival*

Philip Kapleau, *Three Pillars of Zen: Teachings, Practice, and Enlightenment*

Shakta Kaur Khalsa, *Kundalini Yoga: Unlock Your Inner Potential Through Life-Changing Exercise*

Robert Kiyosaki, *Rich Dad Poor Dad: What the Rich Teach Their Kids About Money that Poor and Middle Class Do Not!*

Sandra Maitri, *The Spiritual Dimension of the Enneagram: Nine Faces of the Soul*

Dan Milliman, *The Way of the Peaceful Warrior: A Book That Changes Lives,* also: *No Ordinary Moments: A Peaceful Warriors Guide to Daily Life* and *The Hidden School: Return of the Peaceful Warrior*

Dr. Sue Morter, *The Energy Codes: The 7-Step System to Awaken Your Spirit, Heal Your Body and Live Your Best Life.*

Caroline Myss, *Sacred Contracts: Awakening Your Divine Potential, Anatomy of the Spirit, Why People Don't Heal and How they Can,* and *The Science of Medical Intuition*

Michael Newton, Ph.D. *Journey of Souls: Case Studies of Life Between Lives*

John O'Donohue, *Anam Cara: A Book of Celtic Wisdom* and *Eternal Echoes: Celtic Reflections on Our Yearning to Belong*

Robert Oerter, *The Theory of Almost Everything: The Standard Model, the Unsung Triumph of Modern Physics*

Dean Radin, PhD, *Real Magic: Ancient Wisdom, Modern Science, and a Guide to the Secret Power of the Universe*

James Redfield, *The Celestine Prophecy: An Adventure*

Bruce Rosenblum and **Fred Kuttner,** *Quantum Enigma: Physics Encounters Consciousness*

Don Miguel Ruiz, *The Four Agreements*

Inna Segal, *The Secret Language of your Body: The Essential Guide to Health and Wellness*

Neil Strauss and **Kevin Hart,** *I Can't Make This Up: Life Lessons*

Shunryu Suzuki, *Zen Mind, Beginner's Mind: Informal Talks on Zen Meditation and Practice*

Ellen Tadd, *The Infinite View: A Guidebook for Life on Earth*

Bobby Lake Thom, *Spirits of the Earth: A Guide to Native American Nature Symbols, Stories, and Ceremonies*

Doreen Virtue and **Grant Virtue**, *Angel Words: Visual Evidence of How Words Can be Angels in Your Life* and *Divine Magic: The Seven Sacred Secrets of Manifestation*

Kenneth Wapnick, Ph.D., *The 50 Miracle Principles of A Course in Miracles*

Alan Watts, *Out of Your Mind: Tricksters, Interdependence, and the Cosmic Game of Hide and Seek*

Cynthia Williams, *The Eye of the Dolphin: A Reluctant Journey to Spiritual Awakening and Weirdness*

Sara Wiseman, *Writing the Divine: Experience 33 Lessons for Divine Guidance*

Anton Zeilinger, *The Dance of Photons: From Einstein to Quantum Teleportation*

GRATITUDE

WRITING THIS BOOK HAS BEEN a cathartic experience. Gratitude is the attitude I feel. Somehow, I have been blessed with the time to sit down and contemplate the meaning of my life. More than one thing had to go right in my life to write this book. The stars had to align, and I had to open my heart. I had to let go of the stresses and daily sacrifices. I had to get out of my head and fall into my heart.

First and foremost, I want to thank my wife Flavia Williams. Over this last year you have been gracious and kind. You have shown me true patience and love as I have stepped back and decided to write this book on a whim. You have stepped up and helped keep everything running smooth as I indulged myself and focused on self-care. I know it hasn't always been easy being married to me. I know I have tested the strength of our relationship time and time again. I want you to know that I love you. I want you to know I appreciate everything you do for me and for our family. We are team Flandy and there would be no book without you!

To my mother and my personal angel who brought me into this world I want to thank you. I didn't share many stories about us in this book because the times I have spent with you have all been wonderful. Your gentle hands have shaped my life. You are the kindest, sweetest heart I have ever met. I am lucky to have a mother like you and your grandkids are lucky to have a grandmother so full of love. Thank you for all that you have done and continue to do.

To my Father, I forgive you for anything you and I have clashed heads over. Despite our differences in life, I know that you and I are very similar. Know that I am sorry for the gray hairs I put on your head. When it came down to it, you have always been there for me when needed. You have a heart of gold that I am sure mom has a lot to do with. Thank you for your patience and love. I look forward to collaborating on a book with you!

To my children, I want you to know that my heart is full of love for you. So much that I would gladly lay my life down for any one of you. I hope you don't read these words until you are old enough to understand them. I hope you learn from my mistakes and avoid the pitfalls of life. I will always be here for you even when I am not around. Having the responsibility of raising you three has been my life's greatest joy.

To Jan Whalen, you have been simply amazing. You have shaped and edited my crazy rambling thoughts into something worth reading. You are a strong fierce woman. Thank you for your brutal honesty and your sincere help. Working with you has been a blessing in and of itself. I couldn't ask for a better person to trust my inner thoughts with. You truly are a book Shepard and I look forward to our next adventure.

To Carol of Bella Media Management, thank you! You have also helped shape my thoughts into a book I am proud of. The cover art and design has me bouncing for joy, like a child with a new puppy. You have edited, polished and formatted this book and far exceeded my expectations.

The connection I now feel in my life to everyone and everything is humbling. I feel I can't take credit for the words that poured out of me at times. It was like a higher presence or a higher self pouring a waterfall of information over me. I needed to write this book to unblock the trapped energy I felt within. Now that I have done so, now that I have set my intentions to help others and myself evolve and become more aware, I am in the place and time where the unknown is. Life is unfolding before me and I am simply grateful to be here witnessing it as a member of the pack.

ABOUT THE AUTHOR

Andrew Williams is a father of three beautiful children and husband to a beautiful Brazilian goddess who constantly keeps him in check. He successfully climbed the corporate ladder, then branched out to work as a self-employed real estate investor/ broker. Occasionally, he dabbles in his passion as an independent author/publisher—although this is currently more of a hobby than a career. Known to play the guitar badly while contemplating the depth of daily sacrifice, Andrew is a wanderer. He is a lone wolf who has found a pack at last.

CONNECT WITH THE AUTHOR

In 2019 I have faced down a lot of my demons—depression and anxiety at the top. By sharing this story, I hope to inspire others to conquer their own demons. For any additional help I can provide, please email me at the address below.

Awilliamsteam@gmail.com

Made in the USA
Middletown, DE
19 April 2021